S0-ATA-077

1973

DATE DUE

The Aging Game

Barbara Gallatin Anderson

THE AGING GAME

Success, Sanity, and Sex after 60

McGRAW-HILL BOOK COMPANY

New York   St. Louis   San Francisco
Mexico   Toronto   Düsseldorf

Book design by Anita Walker Scott.

Printed in the United States of America.

Library of Congress Cataloging in Publication Data
Anderson, Barbara Gallatin.
  The aging game.
  Includes bibliographical references and index.
  1. Old age—United States. 2. Aged—United States.
3. Aged—Psychology. I. Title.
[DNLM: 1. Aging. 2. Mental health—In old age. 3. Sex behavior—In old age. WT150 A545a]
HQ1064.U5A649   301.43'5   79-18293
ISBN 0-07-001760-3

Published in association with
SAN FRANCISCO BOOK COMPANY.

123456789 D O D O 7832109

FOR

Edward Franklin Gallatin

Contents

Preface

When Paula Sullivan's husband came home at midnight, petulant and drunk for the third time in as many weeks, and hovered menacingly over her, the five-foot-two, sixty-seven-year-old woman got out of bed, picked up the 200-pound man, and threw him out of their second-story bay window. Two hours later when I talked with her at the hospital—where her sober husband was being put back together again—I asked her why she'd done it and how on earth she had managed the incredible feat. She sat there in a cotton housedress, her hands folded in her lap, and smiled gently at me. "That's easy," she said. "I got angry."

Anger has fallen into disfavor with many psychologists. We are taught to channel our aggressive tendencies "more productively," told that anger is corrosive and futile, that it needs to be sublimated or siphoned off through rigorous exercise. I am not so sure. Anger shakes the complacent. Anger gets things done.

In any case, this is an angry book. I got angry when, in my work as an anthropologist, I saw the efficiency with which our culture destroys in most men and women their potential for happiness and self-respect in late life. I thought that wrong. I thought it an absurd and fruitless posture, devastating to everyone—young *and* old. And I thought it high time for the old, in particular, to abandon their doormat approach to life. I wrote this book.

It is a book about tactics, tactics which if mastered will assure for just about any man or woman in the United States today a successful old age. It speaks to those who will be old. And it tells those already old how to go about changing lives that are unhappy or self-destructive into independent lives that are rich and happy. It considers the physical, intellectual, and emotional assaults that are most common in late life and identifies the resources and alliances through which they are most effectively combated.

The approach that this book advocates is based on copious research. It is not a treatise on positive thinking, based largely on hearty exhortations to get out there and win. You *can* win at the aging game but not without preparation, not without knowledge of the price of acquiescent vulnerability. You have to stop walking into the enemy camp with the conviction that at heart they are basically friendly people.

I haven't the courage of the late Jules Henry, who in the preface to his book *Culture Against Man* acknowledged by name the foundations which had refused to support his research, but I do happily acknowledge a great debt to the National Institute of Mental Health, which supported mine. Southern Methodist University in Dallas, Texas, generously gave me time to write this book.

My major debt is to the men and women on whose life histories this book is based. I have camouflaged their identities. Among them was an ex-prizefighter whose speech at seventy was still liberally sprinkled with the jargon of the ring. When I told him I was writing a book about aging, he clenched his fists and raised them to his chin, his arms pressed close against his body. He jabbed a fist out in mock attack. "Better tell them to be ready for the bell," he said. "And I don't mean the tenth round, either." In the aging game the first round comes earlier than you think. And, in the words of Edward Gallagher, alias Eddie Smith, alias the Frisco Kid: "Fight clean. But if they hit you below the belt—pulverize 'em." This book intends to show you how.

B.G.A.

Oakland
August 1979

The Aging Game

Introduction

In the United States today you can talk about cancer, homosexuality, or rape more easily than you can about aging. During the years I researched the problems of old San Franciscans, the most common question put to me from professionals and friends alike was "Isn't it awfully depressing?" My enthusiasm for my work was considered peculiar if not masochistic. At first I was bothered by these reactions. After a while, however, I began to recognize in them the transparency of most Americans' concern about the passing of youth. I had become a kind of typhoid-Mary, contaminating and ghoulish in my protracted association with the elderly.

I do not exaggerate. At best, late life in the United States today is regarded as an inherently embarrassing development, a greater advance on the scientific frontier than is welcome on the social one. Life after sixty is considered a devalued extension of middle age. A hopeless holding action. As a consequence society is bent on the isolation or planned obsolescence of men

1

and women over sixty. And most old people, deep down inside, come to accept the consensus that they are of little worth.

How absurd. How have we managed to cultivate such a posture? Better still, how can we *un*-cultivate it? We'd better. And quickly. The most recent report of the United States Senate's Special Committee on Aging has signaled "the graying of America." With an excitement unmatched since the assault on compulsory retirement, its members herald a milestone: in 1979 the ratio of post-sixty-five men and women to "young" Americans has reached one in nine. And a monumental increase in their numbers is projected until by the year 2025—in less than a half-century—every *sixth* American will incontrovertibly have left youth behind.

A king-sized challenge if ever there was one. When it comes to the inevitable process of aging, we have stacked the deck so that the odds are heavily against a happy old age for any of us. Why that is the case and how one can go about reducing those odds is what this book is about.

The achievement of success, sanity, and sex after sixty is no mean accomplishment. Today 25 per cent of all suicides in the United States are by men and women over sixty. There is a 30 per cent higher mortality rate among retired persons as compared with employed persons of the same age. And one in five will wind up in a nursing home, most often simply because we do not want them living in our homes and communities. Boredom, depression, and a sense of obsolescence are major problems for the majority of our nation's old.

But it doesn't have to be that way. There *is* a way of beating the house, of living happily though American and no longer young. And the earlier in life that way is recognized and mastered, the better the odds in the aging game. The basic strategies emanate from the experiences of men and women already old. This book simply orders their insights into a practical, working formula for aging. It is the product of three years of anthropological research that compared the lifestyles of 600 residents of San Francisco and its suburbs with those of 600 men and women of the same geographic area who had entered a psychiatric ward for the first time in their lives because of age-linked mental illness. All were over the age of sixty. Eighty persons were studied in depth (forty from each group), not once but in three separate encounters—at least a year apart—by teams of physicians, psychiatrists, sociologists, psychologists, and anthropologists. The files on each of these intensively analyzed individuals reached encyclopedic scope.

My eventual contribution was the co-authorship of an anthropological study of culture and aging, written primarily for specialists in aging. We had indeed learned something of what life is like in the United States for men and women over sixty. Our findings, however, were not destined to be read by the people for whom the message had most significance—Americans themselves.

There was nothing in our findings that restricted their use to scholars. On the contrary, it seemed to me that the insights we had so laboriously achieved should be shared with men and women of all ages, from all walks of life. I wanted to speak to others who are old, to those who live with or know and care about old people, and to those who at fifty or forty or thirty have the uneasy feeling that they are leaving youth and life behind. I wanted to tell this audience what we had learned and what I thought could powerfully and wonderfully change their lives.

What has emerged is a formula for success, sanity, and sex after sixty.

They tell it best—the 1,200 men and women who generously shared with me their most intimate insights into the fight for survival—what it is like to be over sixty in the United States today. In stories of courage and travesty, of humor and despair, these men and women, sick and well, show us how to survive in a rigged and perilous universe or be consumed by a system that is unforgiving of the one in nine Americans who, like Amy Peabody and Angelo Alioto and Maude Simpson, will commit the cardinal sin of growing old.

I

THE ODDS AND
THE CHALLENGE

Later on when she could talk about it, Amy Peabody said that it had begun as an extraordinary day. One of those late November mornings when the sun takes on a sudden vigor and San Francisco's fog melts into a golden warmth. She woke without weariness, took a long careful time for her make-up, and at the last minute changed into a bright yellow suit. She felt buoyant. It was the first time in a long while.

At sixty-five, Miss Peabody had the figure a woman of forty-five might envy, fashionably small and lithe. Her legs were still very good and virtually unmarred, and—though it took too much of her salary—she was always scrupulously groomed and dressed.

"I don't like dowdy styles," she told me. "Most of my noon hours go to browsing the shops or getting my hair done. Lunch out is too expensive anyway."

She *was* young. She had herself and the world convinced of it, she was sure. A few things were tiresome. She always had to wear scarves or thick strings of pearls at her neck, and every morning she rubbed a special cream on the backs of her hands to mask the thick polka dots of age spots. And there were days when she avoided too bright light or sitting beside wide-eyed young things in the cafeteria. But today was not one of them.

From her office in the financial district of San Francisco, she could see the Bay's wind-swept surface turn bright blue. She typed rapidly, with a kind of elation, not even stopping for coffee, and by eleven she had Mr. Connors' brief within a half-dozen pages of completion. He would be pleased. She liked to be thought capable. She *had* to be thought capable.

Things were working out again after a long, wretched stretch of bad luck. She walked by the personnel office and the manager turned abruptly away when their eyes met. He was a meticulous, tenacious little man and he had caused her some dreadful sleepless nights. There was something offensive about his curiosity, his silence, sitting there pouring over information as private as an embrace. Miss Peabody walked wide of the personnel files as she might a coiled snake. For a long while she had thought herself in trouble. And she had felt something close to panic when, yesterday, as she put on her coat to leave, she could feel the little man's eyes on her. She had had a feeling then that he *knew*.

But nothing had happened yesterday or today so far, and at noon she decided to reward herself with a new hat. It was expensive and beautiful, and it made her feel very young.

Miss Peabody had been subtracting years from her age since she was forty. It began with a rather protracted period of being forty-two, an age she still considers ideal.

"You're at a kind of zenith of development then.

Skin, eyes, hair, body—still very good. Enough along to convey stature and sophistication, but not, well, not *too* far along."

Old is a word she can scarcely say, let alone identify with. "I never think of myself *that* way. I have seen what it means, what it does. Old is a dreadful thing to be. I've always had rather a horror of it, I guess."

By the time she was sixty she had lopped a good eight years off her age. At sixty-five she got her job with Mr. Connors, member of a large firm of attorneys. She had said she was fifty-six.

Lying about her age had not been difficult.

"I just really *think* I'm that age. That's what I do. And I *am* a good legal secretary. I have always received top-flight wages. Why, at the height of the Depression I was making more money than my brother Ben was making as a teacher. And I love to work. To be with people. To have my days busy. To me it's exciting to see stacks of things to be done and convert chaos into order."

Her work has taken her all over the United States. "I love to go, go, go. There was a man who wanted to marry me and I loved him. But I didn't and I haven't regretted it. The thought of being tied down some-where . . . I don't know. Work opened doors, took me everywhere, out of a tedious and strict home. It has been my life."

Her present job was one she had fallen into by a stroke of luck after a long period of unemployment. *That* had badly shaken her. It was not the first time in recent years she had been without work, but it was the longest.

"Jobs had somehow begun to tighten up. I started working out of agencies that specialize in temporary jobs." But even they got harder to get. "Silly little jobs I wouldn't have considered even five years ago. I used to

7

get dressed in the morning and go downtown and maybe spend the whole day at some employment office, sitting around waiting for someone to talk to me." She had the first of "real blue spells."

"I'm like an old fire horse. I'd wait around the financial district until five o'clock, mingle with the crowds, and walk up Columbus Avenue, watching the people hop the cable cars and buses. Foxy, the newsman, always had a paper for me."

They usually exchanged a word or two.

"Then, one night when I'd been out of work a long time, he said, 'Hang on old girl. We'll see a hundred yet!' Foxy! He's eighty if he's a day. I went home and stretched out on my bed in all my clothes and I was afraid. It was a very bad time. Once, when I couldn't sleep, I got up and took two sleeping pills. I didn't wake up until ten-thirty."

Periods of unemployment became longer than periods of work, and she struggled to keep up her wardrobe and her pattern of living.

"I couldn't give up my apartment and I even kept Millie, who has cleaned for me for years. But I asked her to come every two weeks instead of weekly. I love Russian Hill. I can see the bridges and the neighborhood is wonderful. Little by little I've acquired some nice things and they're perfect here. I'd die in one of those grim little Bush Street places where the sun never comes and you can't see anything but the house in front of you or a lightwell."

She lost ten pounds. "I just couldn't eat."

When the call came to replace a legal secretary who had had a baby, the understanding was that it would be for two months. "She was supposed to return but she didn't. Somehow I just stayed on. We never really talked about it. That was a year ago. I don't think he'd ever have hired me on a permanent basis. It just goes to show."

With her age listed officially as fifty-six, she still had nine good years before retirement, something she could not bring herself "even to think about." This job was her lifeline, a last tremulous link to life, the only kind of life she knew.

And then it came. In another five minutes she would have picked up her purse and the small gray hatbox and been on her way. She thought of that later, in tortured fantasies of what might have been. Mr. Connors had put it off until the last minute. He didn't buzz for her, but opened the door and asked her to come in.

She knew when she looked at him. Something was very wrong. The first words were hard to get out, but then his voice picked up the familiar slow pattern of studied dispassion that she knew so well. She had the eerie feeling that, with her notebook in her hand, she should be writing very fast or she would lose it all.

He wanted proof of her age, and he asked for it in a way that made it clear no proof would be forthcoming. There were rules about retirement and regulations about insurance. And everyone was desolate, but that was the way it was.

"It's my fault," he said. "I didn't think."

She couldn't think of anything to say. All of a sudden, it would somehow have been comedy to protest.

"It isn't your work, you know," said Mr. Connors. "You're the best." The words went on. Absurd words, for he was firing not promoting her. He gave her a letter of recommendation and a check. Someone else had taken that letter. Someone else knew. The office knew. She wondered how many had watched and known as a silly old lady floated back from lunch, smiling about a new hat and the warm November sun.

It was dark when they left and she refused Mr. Connors' offer of a lift. Later she couldn't remember having said one word, but she must have said something. He looked relieved. At the corner she turned and saw him dart into a popular little bar, noisy now with lively people who were glad it was Friday.

Miss Peabody walked up Columbus Avenue, took Foxy's paper, and climbed the long Union Street hill. Inside her apartment she hung up her coat and opened the hatbox. The sky was almost black now, but on the Bay she could see the Larkspur ferry churning up white water between the bridges.

Amy Peabody opened the window and sailed her hat out into the night. Then she went to the medicine chest and took twelve sleeping tablets. After a while she stretched out on her bed, in her bright yellow suit.

Survival after sixty. It is not easy for over twenty-four million Americans who, like Miss Peabody, are sixty-five or older; a number equal to the combined populations of twenty-one states. They constitute an ever-accelerating proportion of the general population, having increased in numbers sevenfold since 1900 as compared with a threefold increase for the under-sixty group. And the man or woman who lives to seventy can normally anticipate another decade of life, whereas as recently as 1900 those who lived to be forty-nine had exceeded their anticipated allotment of years.

For the first time in history there exist in large numbers men and women already aged by established standards, who have before them ten to twenty more years of healthy life. And we don't know what to do with them. We have created a new social group. Yet the culture which spawned this increase has yet to complete the job and incorporate them into the continuity of society.

We find our old people cumbersome, intrusive, and embarrassing. The consensus is clear. We would be better off without them. Only man among the species applies such consummate skill to the social destruction of his own membership at the same time as he pursues, with scientific relentlessness, the prolongation of life itself. It makes no sense.

For post-sixty Americans, life is a stacked deck. And they can as happily entertain the suggestion that they are growing old as they can the early indications of malignancy. The effect is about the same in society's judgment. Old age is antithetical to acceptance by oneself or others. It is the end of life. At sixty!

As a consequence, few Americans even *want* to prepare for the period that will come to the great majority of us. And by the time we must join them, we are—like Miss Peabody—caught in our own absurdities, and it becomes extremely difficult to imagine that there can be anything but isolation and loneliness in the years we have relegated to ourselves as old people.

But it doesn't have to be. Now, in the lives of many of our old we see a surging, restless yearning for something more, for something better, an alternative to the muted world of lonely hotels and the vacuum of rest homes.

The cleaning woman found Miss Peabody. She had forgotten her sweater and come back to the still, dark apartment. In fifteen minutes the ambulance carrying Amy Peabody to General Emergency roared up and down the hills, plunging in and out of the thick knots of cars, and at Broadway a great crescendo of sound shrieked through the Russian Hill tunnel.

Angelo Alioto heard the siren in his small hotel room and automatically made the sign of the cross, whisper-

11

ing the little prayer he had learned from the Salesian Fathers a half-century before: "St. Joseph, blessed patron of the dying, deliver us from death if it be God's holy will."

Across the table from him, eighty-one-year-old Maude laughed out loud. "Play cards," she said. "Even God can't help you if you keep making stupid moves like that." They played an old Italian version of hearts he had taught her and she beat him with distressing regularity.

She was small and round as he was, but heavily wrinkled. They could almost have passed for mother and son. At sixty-three Angelo called her "old girl" and referred to her as his "girl friend," though there were times when he felt infinitely older. He had grown more dependent than he would have thought possible on her company, her teasing, her ability to lift him out of his blue moods.

After another hand he pushed the cards into the center of the oil-clothed table.

"Seven o'clock. You hungry?"

On Friday, on a good night like this, everybody would be out. They would go to Bozo's, a little bar-restaurant in a sidestreet just above Chinatown where Angelo bought the twisted black cigars he liked and where there would be good baked bass. His girl friend's room was directly below his and she went down now to redo her hair and put on her good coat.

Angelo went to the cupboard and took out a bottle of whiskey. He poured himself a straight shot, and then, before putting it back again, a second. He decided to change his shirt.

The dresser was the only piece of painted furniture in the room. Over it hung a small oval mirror with a matching frame. He had regretted painting them green because the ceiling light gave the color a sickly yellow cast. In a polished silver frame on his dresser was a picture of him in his gray chauffeur's uniform. He had parted his hair on the side then and it was very black. It was not until he was fifty that the gray had come, but then quickly, and at fifty-eight when he last "drove" the black was only a peppering. But his hair had stayed thick and he combed it now with great care.

The walls were a faded swirl of beige-and-white wallpaper that had once been flocked but had thinned to plaster behind the radiator and around the light switch. The curtains were equally colorless and there were no draperies, only green shades at the two small windows, one of which looked out on a rusted fire escape. The other reflected the bright neon sign of Columbus Savings Company. By local hotel standards the cupboard was lavish—polished walnut, a mass of beveled glass and small drawers. It seemed out of place in the small suite where the only kitchen facilities were a two-burner stove and a small sink in a five-by-three-foot alcove. Beyond the brass bed an odd-shaped bathroom thrust alongside the lightwell. Two thick robes hung on the door. Sometimes the card games lasted late and when it was cold he tucked Maude into one of these. The only wall decoration was a picture of Our Lady of Fatima, a present from his brother a long time ago.

When Maude was ready, she tapped once on the ceiling with a double length of broom handle that Angelo had rigged up for her as a signaling device. Whenever she came in she tapped twice on the ceiling to let him know she was there. When she got into bed she tapped out a little dum-dah-dum-dum to which he would respond with a good-night "dah-dah." Three taps meant she needed him and she used it sparingly.

13

Sometimes, if he thought too long about it, he didn't feel like going out at all. "Without the girl friend," he told himself, "I guess I pretty soon wouldn't move."

On weekends he took her for long drives. She seemed never to have been anywhere and he delighted in pointing out the sights in Marin County and down the San Francisco Peninsula. Once they drove as far as Sonoma and went wine-tasting. When he felt the steering wheel in his hands and looked back at the long rear seat, it was almost as though he were driving again. And he wished he were in his uniform.

Now they walked along the "avenue." You didn't see many of the *big* cars anymore. Not even around Union Square where the long limousines used to line up for hire. He had done that kind of driving for a brief period in his early twenties, in partnership with a Filipino who was a real hustler and wound up managing a large-scale rental business. Maybe if he'd stayed with him he would be wealthy today. He didn't know. He'd lost touch.

He loved cars and liked chauffeuring, but he had wanted steady work. He found it at thirty-two with the Cuneos, a wealthy third-generation Italian family in Pacific Heights. At forty-seven he married a thirty-four-year-old teacher whose love was a source of wonder to him. They enjoyed their small home and Angelo was shattered by her death from cancer twelve years later. He began to drink a little more, not heavily, but more often whiskey than wine—though never, he insisted, "when I was to drive." He was increasingly uneasy alone and the Cuneos were supportive and patient.

But when the aging Cuneos finally decided to sell their large house and move into a downtown apartment, Angelo understood. The pattern of life was changing in San Francisco and cabs made more sense

14

now for their rarer excursions. At sixty-two Angelo found his hotel in the area he had known as a young man.

Maude remembered the day he moved in. "I thought he had the wrong address," she said. "He looked like a dandy with a pearly gray hat and a suit you could tell was expensive. This is no hole, but he could have done a lot better. I don't think he knew why he was here himself."

But after a while Maude knew.

"He thinks of himself as a loner, which is a lot of rubbish. The Cuneos were like a second family and he had a lot of friends in those days. Now the Cuneos are gone and about the only one of the old gang around is Vattuoni. His place is down by the old Simmons factory site, and all that is turning into high rise. Very expensive."

Angelo struggled to bring order to his days, to days increasingly without substance.

"He's an early bird," Maude said. "I could hear him at seven in the morning. The sound of water and the sound of shoes. At quarter of eight he'd be down on the street."

Angelo talked about it. "What did I do? Oh, big decisions. I'd stand in the doorway and decide whether to go up Vallejo Street where the coffee is good but the eggs are lousy, or down Green where the eggs are okay but the coffee tastes like burnt oil. After breakfast I'd go up and look at the activity around the big markets, watch the men set up the fruit and the little shops open up. Sometimes I walked down to see Vattuoni. And we'd watch the construction down by the Wharf.

"Once in a while I hopped a bus to Foster's or Compton's for lunch, but mostly I would get a sandwich made at the delicatessen and eat it at home. If I didn't

15

fall asleep after lunch, I walked some more. I don't like to watch TV until nighttime. At about six-thirty I have my big meal. No point going to bed before twelve. I don't sleep that much."

He met Maude when he came home in the rain one night, drunk and chilled. She helped him to bed, and in the morning when his temperature was high she got a doctor to come out to see him and nursed him until he was well again.

Maude started fixing meals for the two of them in her little kitchen. She kept an eye on him and bullied and shamed him into activity. They went to movies and she fished with him at Aquatic Park and played cards in his room where they could catch the ten o'clock news on television.

"Eighty-one," Angelo said, in wonder and respect. "She calls herself a rest-home refugee and she's a fighter. I looked at her and I looked at myself and I decided it wasn't time to lie down yet."

They were rarely apart now, and on nice nights like this Angelo found himself planning for the future.

"I was thinking what a kick she'd get if maybe I bought a little cabin up in the Gold Country where she lived as a kid. We're going to take some rides and look around."

Once in a while the blue spells come back and he takes "a drink or two." But he hasn't been drunk in more than a year.

Now, when they had come back from dinner, his girl friend fixed them both a coffee-royale and he sat across from her in the small room, watching her twist a piece of lemon into the cups, smelling the clean, pungent odor. He felt pretty good. He was learning. Something that she knew he was just beginning to understand

16

and to make his own too. Something to do with life, not death; with the beginning and not the end of things.

In a sudden gesture, he lifted his arm and clenched a fist to the ceiling.

"Saint Peter," he said, "you got to wait a little while longer."

Maude laughed out loud, and he added: "For the two of us."

Look at it this way. Surviving successfully, though old, in the United States today involves a special kind of mastery, of know-how, a brand of pioneer. A Maude.

The old must face an unsympathetic, often hostile, world and wring happiness from it. They must demand and find an honorable place in it. They must defend their right to continuing identification with the living though society tries to shunt them into its euphemistic outposts to death—rest homes and retirement communities—or, at best, social isolation. And the tacit, unexamined, "logical" nature of society's hostility makes coping with it all the more dangerous.

Aging in the United States today is for every individual a challenge that calls to mind the mastery associated with judo or karate. It suggests an unevenly weighted encounter. It demands the acquisition of skills needed to cope with an opponent of superior advantage or strength. Special, definitive, isolable skills. The poor odds inherent in any such confrontation discourage many old people. Yet they should not, if only because there really is not an acceptable alternative to the struggle. Maude knew it. You can fight against great odds and risk defeat. Or, you can *not* fight and *accept* defeat. The fight itself buys time, builds self-esteem, develops resources, and with the proper preparation holds more

17

promise than the old realize. In any case, when you start from the premise of social worthlessness, the old do not have much to lose in an out-and-out confrontation. Especially not if they were to do it in numbers, maximizing their strengths.

Ideally, it is best to anticipate the struggle and marshal resources. And the time to arm is before the cold morn of the retirement party. Yet men and women of seventy, and older, can make the decision that they will be pushed no longer into becoming social zombies to salve the conscience of a discomforted society, and *do* something about it.

Maude was seventy when she walked out of an Oakland convalescent home arid took a bus to San Francisco.

"I had been asking to leave for six months and no one listened to me—not my family or the hospital or the doctor. I had a valise and a twenty-dollar bill and a big, fat contempt for the system that put me there.

"No one had seen me in a coat since they had wheeled me in ten months before, after gall-bladder surgery. I pulled my hat down and walked out with a bunch of people when visiting hours were over."

She laughed. "It was like a jail break."

She recalled her timid two-block walk to the bus stop. "My legs were like Jell-O and I didn't feel at all brave. But there wasn't anything *wrong* with me. In any case, I hadn't seen a doctor in six weeks. I just had to get away and I knew it would never be any easier."

The bus driver deposited her in downtown San Francisco after a drive across the San Francisco Bay Bridge that "was glorious. Just glorious. I saw people reading papers and carrying packages and talking to one another. People with places to go and things to do. And I wondered if they knew about the secret worlds—how

18

many there must be—where time and motion stand still, where nothing happens or ever can happen. I smiled at everyone. Like a person reprieved from death."

She knew where she was going. To a little rooming house a friend of hers had once stayed in.

"It was run by a German couple, way out on California Street. I used to talk to them when I visited her and I figured that if they couldn't take me they'd find me something. I gave them the twenty as an advance on a month's rent, and then I phoned my daughter."

The convalescent home had already called her daughter.

"Once sick, always sick, that's what *she* thought. That gall-bladder operation was like a sentence to suspended animation. Somehow I was supposed never to have any other home again. It was simply more convenient for everyone that I stay there, though I don't think they ever actually said it—even to themselves."

But Maude was ready. She'd been ready for a long time. "Why do we have to be problems to be worked out, like some national disaster?

"I said to my daughter, 'Look. I'm not sick or helpless or insane, but I will be if I have to spend any more days in a *rest* home. I'm not ill, I'm just not as young as I used to be. And I've had enough rest to last me for another ten years.'

"I had thought it all out. It was not an impulsive move."

Her husband had worked for the State of California and had left a small lifetime pension which would now come to her, not the rest home, and she had a bit of land in the country that was surely worth something.

"I couldn't think of a better time to find out just how much. And the money has done me a lot more good than it ever would my heirs, regardless of what they think."

Maude stayed with the German couple until the rooming house changed hands. In her seventy-eighth year she moved to her present hotel on Stockton Street, where she eventually met Angelo.

"North Beach has always appealed to me. You're close to downtown and Fisherman's Wharf and there's always something to see. I like it best where there's action. Where life is."

Maude knew it intuitively. Successful aging requires strategy. It can no more be left to chance than can a military campaign be left to the vagaries of the enemy. And, before any kind of aging strategy can be mapped, decisions must be made, and not lightly. These involve, first of all, commitment—the kind of commitment that precedes a successful diet. Success in aging is impossible without absolute, unqualified personal honesty. Honesty with self, that is. Honesty with society is obviously ill advised in so uneven a struggle as aging in America. If you are going to take on society at the present odds, you must be totally committed to a no-retreat confrontation. There can be no carefully planned loopholes for graceful retreat when the going gets rough.

Secondly, each individual must get to know the environment, the battlefield on which the combat of survival as an old person takes place daily. Then decisions can be made about tactics. In a broad sense this means that men and women must come not only to understand but to *realize* on a personal level that America's most fundamental values are antithetical to a high position for the aged.

Americans prize youth, productivity, and independence. More accurately, Americans have learned to live with a static image of themselves as young, productive, and independent. It is this imagery that they somehow expect to sustain, unsullied by change, across the life span. The more it is assailed—as it must be—by time and circumstance, the more vehemently it is defended. This means that as a nation we devalue, and therefore shun, the obsolescent, the inactive, and the dependent. Retired or dependent "senior citizens" haven't a chance. As Mr. Shuey, a sixty-one-year-old ex-advertising man put it: "Valuewise, we're the pits. You can sell an old mattress easier than you can an old executive. It is basically un-American to get old."

Pretending these sentiments are not there is worse than useless. Such pretense imperils and lulls one from the precautions that might otherwise minimize their influence.

Every person younger than sixty is the adversary of every aging American until proven otherwise. Every person. This is simply because they are not yet old. Nor should the old presume certain automatic exceptions: their children, employers, ministers, physicians. The closer the tie the greater the threat, for these are people in extraordinary positions to exert influence on the future of the aged.

Of course the old love their children, may be staunchly devoted to an employer (if they still have one), regard their ministers as their spiritual guides, and place their lives regularly in the hands of their physicians. In these relationships, however, the former primary statuses of parent, employee, parishioner, and patient undergo a metamorphosis in late life. After sixty, the critical status becomes OLD PERSON. And that dimension, OLD, takes precedence socially over everything and anything else. After sixty, you are an old parent, an old employee, an old parishioner, and an old patient.

The majority of old people do not recognize a fundamental concomitant of aging that is immediately apparent to all who are not old. They overwhelmingly do not recognize that they have entered a new life phase. And that is the crux of the problem. The old are "old." It is as simple as that. What they make or fail to make of themselves they must do as old people. And it doesn't matter about comparative modifiers: relatively old (in terms of other old people), in comparatively good health (in terms of people of their own age group), or young in heart (an appalling phrase that suggests old in heart is an awful thing to be). This apprehensive discomfort with the designation "old" is glaringly apparent in the readiness with which old people accept cloying euphemisms—senior citizens, golden-agers, etc.

Youth is in full flood and by cultural acclamation dominates the first two to three decades of life. What we have is a weird kind of distribution. Youth to about thirty, and then a lengthy, amorphous period of what can be called, for want of a more acceptable label, "adulthood"—which stretches in a rather specious plateau from about thirty to sixty, with possible subdivisions of "early" and "late." At sixty, the total population experiences a precipitous drop to "old age." A cultural vestibule, not only to death, but to the final cessation of young life, which we all have learned to treasure fiercely.

Old age has yet to be perceived as a significant life phase so that behavioral cues for the person in passage are ambiguous, often contradictory, and, in the critical area of goals, nonexistent. As a consequence, major problems arise as to how to "behave" in old age. American society has responded by extending the guidelines of middle life virtually intact. It is a simple but unfortunate expedient. The ultimate endorsement, ironically, is provided by the old themselves. They seal their fate by going along with America's assessment of them as deteriorated middle-agers.

Tell the old long enough that they are nothing except in relation to their past, and they will work with dedication to cut off growth and tailor themselves back into an obsolescent mold. And, given the social equation, society can legitimately complain that they are not making it and should either try harder, or, like Miss Peabody, retire permanently from the competition. That's what their children think and, more often than not, their employers, ministers, and doctors. Maude adds: "Sometimes I'm not so sure about God."

The fight America's old must wage is not for a renewal of middle-life status (that's the wrong battlefield), but for standards and status *as old people*. Old age must cease to be a dirty word, and it will be a dirty word for as long as the old are regarded, and are content to be regarded, as overripe adults. It is like calling a man of twenty-five a senile teenager. Actually the battle should be one that engages *all* Americans. Certainly the outcome will affect the destinies of us all.

A view of old age as a downhill slide unfortunately admits of only one course of action—a downhill slide. And then one must somehow live in the bleak terminal at the bottom. It can be done and the choices are as limited as they are unappealing: retrogression and a desperate search for the irretrievable youth; apathy; withdrawal from the painful social reflection of a denigrated self; tedious recitation of past glories, liberally embroidered for weary audiences; baleful self-torture about what might have been.

When enough old people are seriously engaged in

23

shaping a meaningful way of life for themselves as old people, society will be forced to help. Old people will become justifiably proud of their status. A new concept of personal growth in late life will replace our present stultifying conviction of decay and disuse. And successful adaptation to the post-sixty years will become the normal way of life for men and women in the United States.

This goal is predicated on the conviction that right now, today, society can be successfully confronted. That one can be happy though sixty and beyond.

There is a way.

II

THE STRATEGY
OF AGING

Victory in the aging game requires calm but consummate strategy. Specifically, a meaningful way of life for America's old can be accomplished through use of the following tactics:

1. Accept yourself as old;

2. Develop a clear perspective on late life;

3. Replace lost satisfactions;

4. Develop the resources that count; and

5. Develop the alliances that count.

Each of these tactics involves some new ways of thinking and looking at yourself after sixty, and together they make specific demands for new behavior patterns as an old person. They are best faced sequentially, though this is not an inevitable order. All must be worked through. Successful aging is a product of their completion and combination. The pace and style of

25

progress through them will vary widely depending on the insight, drive, and reserves of the individual. But they are closed to no one. Neither great age, sickness, poverty, nor isolation nullifies the promise that late life can be much, much better than it is. Those conditions make it tougher, that's all.

In the following pages, each tactic is considered in terms of approaches and perils. Study of the accumulated experiences of many old people has made possible, even obvious, the identification of this route to successful aging. The success stories are theirs, and real. Even the failures can be drawn upon to insure that they will not be repeated. We can and should learn from them. These men and women are pioneers in the business of growing not just old, but older.

Tactic One:
Accept Yourself as Old

It is one thing to rationalize the deference of the tall man who called you sir, or the woman who offered you her seat on the bus, or to wonder about the absurd proliferation of very young policemen. And one can ignore for surprisingly long the bizarre changes in the bathroom mirror. But retirement, that first social security check, or a sixtieth birthday are straightforward and unmistakable developments. In the United States today the message is loud and clear. You are OLD.

"Old, *old*," said Miss Peabody. "All the time I lay there, I could *hear* it. Like a gong, over and over. I'd rather die."

Miss Peabody could not cope with old age because she never faced it.

Old age is a time of life, a stage to which we all come by virtue of the phenomenon of uninterrupted life. And it makes for quite different perspectives of aging, whether wrinkles and whitening hair are regarded as evidence of fruition and achievement, or of deterioration. In the United States today the only women who can be acceptably gray or white are those too young to be thought old (the Jean Harlows) or too old remotely to be thought young (as in the classic grandma imagery).

It is entirely normal to prefer black hair to gray, and clear, unlined skin to wrinkles. To strive for the former and avoid the latter makes sense as long as the results are satisfying and there is continuing evidence of return on one's investment in time and energy and ego strength. Up to now, however, where this strategy exists it has largely been a part of a general *denial* of aging. We attempt to pass as younger than our years, like youngsters trying to get by the box office and into the theater at privileged rates despite posted age limits. Miss Peabody lied to hospital physicians about her age. Even loss of retirement benefits, better health care, and earned leisure are regarded by some as small sacrifices for the relative benefits of continuing non-old status.

Such behavior, however—even when it works—is basically non-adaptive. In the first place, it has only short-lived utility, delaying identification by some people or minimally diverting the attention of others.

27

But, more significantly, it can never provide the basis for successful aging because it never comes to grips with it. Rather, it reinforces the conviction that what is attractive, what is valued, what is worthy of oneself and society, is whatever removes the individual from the time dimension he or she is in fact entering.

Keeping your chronological age to yourself, particularly during the transitional phase of aging, may be feasible and profitable—a tiny but felicitous advantage in the present rigged cultural universe. What is critical is that you remember what you are about, *really*, recognizing that these are peripheral tactics. And *you*, not America's vast youth-oriented advertising empires, must dictate the wisdom and scope of strategems. For these neither arrest nor seriously delay the challenge of aging. They do not replace nor obviate the critical task of making something of old age itself. Each man and woman should ultimately be concerned with good looks and good body and attractiveness as an *old* person. For the first tactic of successful aging is recognition of the changes that longer life eventually brings to all of us, despite our cleverest efforts.

Rather than a surrender, it is a confrontation and a challenge: to see oneself, to accept oneself, to face society as old. Men and women alike stand a better chance as older Americans from a position of strength based on inventoried assets than on construed liabilities or the consuming burden of self-deceit. It is a mistake to direct the struggle to a continued hold on middle life. The struggle must be waged within the present dimension of life. And its goal should be a new image of aging. A bold, but more rational one. A valued one.

People who cannot accept old age often view themselves as devitalized and offensive to others. They magnify the liabilities of change. These become the lens of

28

self-analysis. Evidence that fails to support these dim views may be totally discounted.

"Some people claim I don't look very different, but I know I do," said a woman of seventy who hid from old friends in growing seclusion. "So ashamed to have someone see you, you grit your teeth. I look like I came out of an old bucket."

Frightened to their souls, suffused with horror in their phobic absorption with aging, these people simply succumb. They succumb to nervousness, fatigue, and chilling despair. Theirs is the what-difference-does-it-make-it-will-only-get-worse attitude. Inertia may outweigh the effort of care—of looks and wardrobes, and often of rudimentary hygiene as well.

"Who cares? Who notices? I know it's not the way to be—but I've become so lazy. It's an effort to brush my teeth."

Some find release in a kind of self-hypnosis that frees them from demands and from introspection. "I have no desire to do anything but close my eyes and go to sleep. I want to lose track of time." And this at a time when vigilance could most enhance a challenged, sometimes fragile ego.

We are talking about a self-fulfilling prophecy. These men and women look ahead and see engulfing deterioration (though it need never come), and then almost scrupulously set in motion the forces that create it. These are people so appalled by the physical change of age that they have lost rational perspective. Unwittingly they sound the knell for the diminution of life. And they find no comfort at all in the fact that these changes come to everyone. Aging is seen as a personal affront.

It seemed an affront to Robert Marshall, a virile widower who at sixty-three was a semi-retired attor-

ney, a tennis buff, and a much sought-after dinner partner. When his first grandchild was born, Marshall's joy
was soon tempered by the suspicion that he was older
than he thought and that his "grandpa" role meant the
beginning of the end of a social world he had thought
secure and changeless. He was unnerved by the well-
meaning joshing of his friends. And when one or two
anticipated invitations were not forthcoming he leaped
to the conclusion that his friends thought him over the
hill and that women were avoiding him.

"I'd heard of people getting worked up about aging,
but I never thought it would happen to me. Why, I
would go into the bathroom and just stare at myself—
the gray hair (getting whiter by the minute) and the line
of my chin and throat. When I smiled I radiated wrinkles, and when I didn't I felt like one massive droop.
Scared the hell out of me. And it would all get worse!
That's what ate at me. How much worse? How fast? You
won't believe it but I'd get sweaty palms and my heart
would pound sometimes."

He kept the depth of his concern to himself. Six
months later when I spoke with his son, he was at a loss
to understand why his father's life had taken the direction it had.

"All of a sudden the starch went out of him. Why
sometimes I'd find him sitting around his apartment at
two in the afternoon, unshaven and still in his pajamas.
Other times we couldn't reach him on the phone for
days. His office would call, all upset because he'd stood
up a client, but mainly worried because it wasn't like
him at all. Nothing was."

It took almost a year of what Robert Marshall called
"the agony route" before he himself sought out private
psychiatric counseling.

"Basically I'm a logical man," he told me. "I could feel sanity slipping away from me. I couldn't be with people, and my home had turned into a prison. I lost twenty pounds. Finally I was plain out of reserve strength and I knew it. I just picked up the phone and called a psychiatrist I'd assisted once in a court case and I told him I sure in hell needed to talk with somebody. He let me come in that afternoon."

When I saw him on the final round of interviewing Marshall's granddaughter was almost three, and he was, in his own words, "out of the woods and back on the courts." He talked easily about the recent past.

"You know, when you're forty or fifty and you see it happen to some old guy, you think: 'What's with him? He doesn't know when he's well off.' And you wonder what's so rough about being sixty and getting out of the rat race. It should happen to you." He hesitated. "But it's different when you get there yourself."

We were sitting on the tiny balcony of his condominium looking down on the marine activity at Aquatic Park in San Francisco. A stiff breeze whipped the flags and sailboats tacked into the wind. Robert Marshall's mood seemed as animated as the sea. "I have a theory," he told me. "I don't think anybody ages 'gracefully.' That's a lot of bull. Some of us keep it inside more than others and that's a mistake, a big mistake, in my judgment. Yell like hell! That's what I say. You want to go on living but you hate to pay your dues."

He poured us both some fresh coffee and sat for a moment with the warm cup in his hands. "I don't know that it had to be as bad for me as it was," he said finally. "It took so long to find my way, to monitor what was happening and learn to revel in the good things, and to

31

shake my fist at what I couldn't change. Life is good again and I'm sure in hell going to keep it that way—even if I live to be a great-grandfather."

He laughed out loud. *"Especially* if I live to be a great-grandfather!"

The most dangerous perspective is associating the changes of age with abnormality (so that gray hair is regarded as inherently abnormal, rather than a predictable late-life body change). In this view there is something *wrong* with being old. There are those who, as a consequence, will not succumb to aging—EVER. They will enter into any kind of battle to halt its physical advance. And a good (and permanent) defense, they believe, is the best offense. These men and women remain middle-aged with a vengeance. On her release from the hospital, Miss Peabody enrolled in charm school. She dressed in youthful styles, wore bright lipstick, and continued to subtract ten to fifteen years from her age as the occasion seemed to demand. She couldn't imagine why, when we were studying old age, we wanted to speak with *her.* Her efforts, however, have had limited success in effecting substantial change in her own self-estimation.

"I don't know what others think. I look in the glass—and well, I keep using the cream they advise. Guess I'm not faithful enough."

In an unguarded moment, she admits it will only get worse. "What am I good for? Nothing. Not now, when you come right down to it. I just keep on living. I keep wishing I could do something. *I wish someone would tell me.*"

Miss Peabody cannot be dismissed as a zany old woman. She simply mirrors, more candidly than most, America's devaluation of the post-sixty years. Throughout her life she has collaborated—unwittingly but devastatingly—with the forces that will destroy her as an old person. That she has done this, for the most part, with ingenious zest makes her a tragic, not comic, figure.

For many old people the actual hang-up in the acceptance of aging is not physical changes, though they talk as though these are the root of all their problems. Bodily changes terrify many largely because these are translated into deterioration of the *self*. The actual, underlying fear is that the "real me" may erode before the aggression of time just as the skin erodes (yields to tonal and circulatory change). Advancing ego suggests to them a weird, impending contagion. Today the body, tomorrow the mind—and the *me*. Deny bodily change and the whole frightful syndrome will be arrested. I am not old. You do me an injustice to associate my destiny with the imminent decay of America's post-sixty population. Old is nothingness. Society says so. And each new day seems to bring some cruel reinforcement of that destiny—of nothingness. Old is de-sexed, de-adventured, soporific sameness. For these men and women, there is rarely a fear of death. Rather, in their apathy, most live as though immortal.

A New Image

To build a positive image you have to begin with some idea of what a good or acceptable or feasible image should be. For most old people, the present image is vestigial of a past self and there is *no* future self.

When asked about herself, Helen Cormoran, a widow and mother of two married sons, remarked: "I don't know myself." Interviewed a year later and asked to describe herself today at sixty-seven, she says: "I don't know—a funny person." The interview is resisted. Obviously she feels threatened by the line of probing. The interviewer then changes tactics and takes her back to a time when a view of the self was a good view. "What were you like at fifty?" In her response the present "old" self emerges too, pale in comparison with what used to be. "I was active, attractive I think. I took interest in life. Now. Now I don't care. I feel I've lived my life. There is no place to go."

The development of a healthy self-image is not an easy task in late life. But unaltered, unadapted, the image of the self that served to sustain in middle life is not only incongruous with the physical evidence of aging, it provides no credible basis for adaptation to daily life as an older American. It is nevertheless an image grudgingly discarded. For the dilemma is this: while it may not be healthy to cling too long to the middle-life self, the conventional public image of the old self is a wretched and stultifying substitute. For most old people, the choice is somewhat like deciding between an outdated, ill-fitting garment and a shroud.

For ninety-three-year-old Cy Hart the years have brought changes. Some grievous. Particularly on the body, on the packaging of the product. And this is not to be denied. But, he emphasizes, the contents are intact. The self is not withering; it has not died. *It has entered a new cycle.* "The crisis came early and I had a very bad time during my early fifties. I blamed it on everything but what it was, a mounting terror of growing old."

We were talking in his studio-bedroom in one of the brick and stucco buildings that abound in San Francisco's Marina District. The divan-type bed extended into a large bay window from which Mr. Hart had an unobstructed view of the heavy bridge-bound Chestnut Street traffic.

"The place has a bedroom," he said, "but since I seem to spend an increasing amount of time under the covers I decided I might as well be in the sunniest room. Also, you'll notice these windows are visible from just about every building around us, and my neighbors—all very solicitous about me—insist they can keep better track of me this way. When I am up or awake the shades are up. If I am asleep or resting I pull them down. My phone rings pretty promptly," he pointed to his nightstand, "if I look as though I'm much off schedule."

Mr. Hart has outlived two of his four children and his three wives—"darling ladies, every one."

"My fifty-fifth birthday hit me like an avalanche," he continued. "I decided that I had about five years of real life left. Drove my sweet, patient wife almost to a divorce, and myself to nervous exhaustion. Wound up, three years later, flat on my back for two months with plenty of time to think. I'd been driving myself in my business, flitting around at night to prove to myself I was still a lady-killer, I guess, and entertaining like a movie magnate."

His second wife was three years older than he, and he recalled now the "stunning knowledge that *she* was sixty. Sixty-one actually, and *I* was making all the noise. I remember that for the first time in months we took the time to talk and be together."

He smiled. "I've been lucky when it comes to women. Lucky in a lot of ways. She just said, 'Cy, if you don't give a little thought to the present, the real present, the doctor says you aren't going to *have* any future. We'd both miss out on a lot, you know."

For Cy Hart "all the pieces fell into place. Why should

35

'sixty' have such a malevolent ring? It's like they say, you don't appreciate something until you think you're about to lose it. I made the decision to live, to enjoy life at my own pace, to look forward to life—as I always had. And I've never regretted it."

Maude put it this way: "I didn't expect to get any younger." *Her* problem was that others apparently thought she should. "When I got sick and was hospitalized, my daughter decided it was the end of the line for me. There was never any real conspiracy to leave me in that convalescent home. In a way that would have been easier to handle. One day, when I spoke about going home, as I fully expected to, my daughter said, 'but Mother, you're seventy-three!' "

As Maude insisted, "I wasn't quite that ready to translate 'old' as 'dead.' "

Cy and Maude have emerged from their confrontations with aging with a dynamic imagery of late life. One to be *lived* with. Without terror and with hope. It is the image of the self as a familiar vital individual, a robust ego, trapped to be sure within the vulnerability of the body, the encircling cycle of physical aging. But that's par for the course, the universal dimension, the price of all life.

"I'm Cy Hart. And that's something that won't change." *Inside, I'm the same me:* This is the message to the self that helps people like Cy and Maude over the rough spots, when they have to cope with the ravages that age has wantonly brought. But these changes, like the fifteen-year-old's acne, are a kind of badge of status, scarcely terminal. "Sure, I'd be glad to be rid of them (the wrinkles)," says one woman of sixty-five. "But you know, it took a hell of a lot of living to make them."

Humor helps. "You got to keep your foot off the panic button," says Mrs. Arensberg, whose many family photographs attest to her great beauty as a young wife and mother.

Some become assiduous tacticians, appraising change and its demands on them. "Physically, I suppose I do look a good fifteen years older than I did at fifty," concedes Gina Rowles, a recent bride. "But I think people forget that I have all those wrinkles. Let them forget." It is as though the aging process were some fascinating kind of evolution taking place before her very eyes. Aspects of it, she admits, are deplorable. She reported being shocked when she got glasses and saw how wrinkled she was. Yet she knows that these changes do not really gain access to the significant *her.*

"I don't know that I've changed in any meaningful way. I don't worry anymore about growing older." And nothing dangerous invades her contentment, much of which she attributes to her second marriage after a disconsolate period of widowhood. She is able to put physical change in perspective.

It is not all easy, and there can be no ready pretense that it is. Yet the ability to look squarely at the liabilities of age makes possible a non-traumatic appraisal of mental change as well.

"You begin to lose some memory capacity as you get older," says a retired teacher. "I'm seventy-five. Forget names, never faces. Not really bad, but damned inconvenient. Something you've got to learn to compensate for. I write down what I want to remember."

Gina, the recent bride, paints this picture of herself: "A bit of a dreamer and sometimes rather childish-minded and overly conservative, particularly about religion and politics. But then I don't know how much of that is old age. Do you know I didn't want Stevenson to be President because he was divorced?"

Asked if his wife has seen changes in him with the

years, Charles Lindsey, a retired salesman, is sensitive to the complexities of aging. "Definitely. All kinds, physical, probably mental. Because there have been changes. Hasn't made any difference, really. It happened to both of us. I still *feel* the same."

This new image of age then must take into account the physical, cognitive, and personality changes that age *does* bring: not in the same measure to all, but in some measure to each of us. It must, at the same time, take into account the integrity and agelessness of the self, the me, the soul, if you are comfortable with that word.

Age is part change and part continuity. It is embodied in the position of an astute man who said: "The doctor says I'm getting old and should increase my fluid intake. I do. I've started taking my Scotch with water instead of straight. You've got to adapt."

Adaptive persons continuously monitor their behavior over time, thus aging "successfully." Americans are heartily eager to label old people as "fixed in their ways." Their assessment, however, would be more credible if they allowed the post-sixty men and women of our culture *alternative* ways. It is a little like deploring a drowning man's firm grip on the rock that saves him from being swept over the falls. Most Americans view the spectacle with stunning dispassion—from the shore.

There is always some environment that is optimal for the age and the state of an organism, an environment in which life can enjoy its fullest potential. The depressed, defensive, sometimes petulant behavior of many old people is a reflection of the frustration they face in their intuitive but fruitless search for that environment. No social group, no age group, sees the world unrelievedly through rose-colored glasses. And the man or woman who makes for monstrous company at sixty was probably no picnic at forty either.

Dividends of Longer Life

What has scarcely been explored is the extent to which old age is a period of personal *growth*, a time when there can develop an improved image of the self, based on positive dividends of longer life.

"My God," said Roy Junniver, "it's a good thing they retired me. Forty years an accountant. I'd never have quit. Eight to five, fifty weeks of the year. I had a mind like a concrete block."

Today he has moved at seventy from amateur to professional status in a newfound activity, developing miniature varieties of garden flowers. After twenty years of widowhood he married a woman he came to know through his new work. He lost thirty pounds, dresses with renewed interest in his appearance, and is currently considering taking on some lecture opportunities.

"I was depressed at first," he says of his retirement. "I thought it was the end of the line, that I'd be old and a nobody. I *was* a nobody and long before I was old. That's what I didn't know. One day recently I went back to the office and I was engulfed again with the old boredom of the life I used to live. A pitiful lot, really."

His broad scoffing suggests occasional sour-grapes relapses, but Junniver is ready to put the past behind him and in the best American tradition look to the rich promise of the future. What is innovative is that he can do it now from the position of an old person, from a new imagery of personal worth. And what is clear is that life at seventy makes more demands upon his potentialities than it ever has and rewards him more bountifully when he rises to those demands. Certainly he is not invulnerable and betrays occasional self-doubt, but as he himself says, "It's too much to ask that everything turn up roses. Six or sixty, a fellow can never demand that. But it looks good. Hell, it looks better than it ever did."

The first tactic of aging, then, is a kind of shifting of gears, a sense of the end of middle age. The critical obligation to accept aging and get on with the business of life. Thinking old and being old gag Miss Peabody. Almost literally. Her body and mind reject—expel—the sick concept of old age. But the "sickness" which attaches to the imagery of the late-life self for most Americans is social in origin, and a distortion of what is, actually, a new phenomenon for mankind: added, special, potentially bountiful years of *life*. What *is* sick is to retreat from that potential because the quality of the new life is in some ways different from life as we have known it.

False starts do not negate the chance for successful aging. "It takes a while to get the hang of it," says Maude. "After all, most of us are sixty for the first time." Or seventy, or eighty.

The willingness to *seek* a meaningful way of life after sixty can only derive from an acceptance of old age—of oneself as old. The next section suggests how this new kind of involvement with life can be launched. It is the second tactic of aging: the shaping of a personal blueprint for life after sixty. From it proceeds the building of the special skills and specific strategies that can make of old age a period of personal growth and of new social identification.

40

Tactic Two: Develop a Clear Perspective on Late Life

By the time a person is sixty he or she has created a personal world as distinct as one's fingerprints. This world is a product of personal experience and social adaptation, the foundation for all building and decay. Within it rests the total product of past life: false starts, proud achievements, disguised failures. It is the computer out of whose vast memory bank present action is projected. It is greater and more abstract than personality. It is less than culture. It is the genetic singularity of the individual—a minute slab of all of culture.

An individual's personal world *is* his or her reality, that private and social stage of all thought, emotion, action, and inaction. It is the monitor of all communication. What is not generally understood is the significant difference between these "worlds" as they exist for the old and for those who are not old. Although no two worlds are precisely the same, some are more alike than others by virtue of common experience and, most importantly, shared status.

But the cultural distinctiveness of the old, in fact, lies precisely in their lack of status. There is basically no role at all for the aged in our society in the sense of positive behavioral expectations. They are expected to be acted upon but not to act. No consensus exists as to how they can continue the fruitful extension and development of their personal worlds, their links with others. The concepts "aged," "old," are ambiguous and damning; they merge the distinctions that are made in most cultures between healthy longevity and that helpless, near-moribund stage that often just precedes death.

Since there is no prescription for living after sixty, the suspicion has taken root that there *is* no life after sixty. The relegation of the old to social death follows as a more or less inevitable and defensible consequence.

With discontinued worlds, the old have become social phantoms. And like phantoms, they make us uncomfortable. We relegate them to white-sheeted habitats where they (and we) will feel more comfortable among their own kind; we send them to golden-age homes, antichambers to eternity. And the implication is that they are dragging their feet. Heaven waits.

If they must live among us, we divorce ourselves emotionally from them. Florida Scott-Maxwell, eminent British psychoanalyst, describes her own reactions as an aging woman. "What we get is an odd experience of anonymity, as though we moved along the cracks between the lives of other people." And she continues: "I know one woman who was once so lovely that as she walked all eyes were on her, and if she turned around others turned to look at her. As she aged she noticed that everyone looked right through her, as though she were not there at all. It gave her a funny sense of freedom, but also a sense that she had become invisible. She felt she could go anywhere, into houses and out again. No one would stop her for no one would see her. She even wondered if she dared dance instead of just walking, but thought it more prudent not to try."

It can come as no surprise that the private worlds of America's old are often vague and lonely places. The quality so many communicate is of being ill defined, out in left field, sitting in a theater when the performance is next door. As a former school teacher put it: "Being old is like having bad breath—a built-in distancing mechanism."

It is not clear when the sense of I-am-expendable comes to the aging American. But at some point it becomes more a conscious than unconscious absorption. Most of us go through life with a sense of immortality, convinced that aging is something that happens to other people. It is not a psychically healthy deception. We build a residence for an eternal self—or better, a self free of the time dimension. We delay scores of undertakings, confident they can be begun at will. With advancing years, however, comes the realization of the fact of death, and simultaneously yet another distancing mechanism between the old and the not-old. For the old the threat is to the vitality of their own personal worlds.

"It's not death I'm afraid of," said Angelo. "It's not living. That's what's killing me." And he laughed out loud at the figure of speech.

Old age brings us to the end of the blueprint for living. For building. And we are builders! Worse, with aging the tendency is for society to encroach more and more, uninvited but with a sense of privilege, upon personal, previously inviolable worlds. Lack of status makes this possible, lowering the no-trespassing signs that protect the worlds of others who are not old.

"I had my own room," said Julia Arensberg, a Polish-born widow, speaking of life in her son's home, "and it was upsetting to everyone when I left it. I had my own cup and plate and my linens were marked with my name. Nobody else's were. When there was company I was fed early with the children and my

43

daughter-in-law would suggest I might like to see a movie. One night when I came home too early and joined them at coffee, my daughter-in-law apologized for my presence to the guests as they left."

Kai Andersen, a robust seventy-year-old, reported that in his daughter's home he alone had fixed hours for showering or bathing. "Also, it was clear that she was happier if I didn't materialize until *everyone* had left the house in the morning, and on weekends ideally I was supposed to be up, *out* of the house, and into the garden before anyone got out of bed. I'd have to lie there and figure out what day it was before I could move. Rainy weekends I'd spend mainly at the neighborhood library." If he didn't talk they accused him of sulking, "but nobody really wanted to talk to me except my grandson. He's eight."

The social jeopardy of the old in intergenerational relations is not necessarily eliminated when they elect to remain in their own residences.

When Hazel Arcero's husband died she offered to share her large Richmond district home with her son and his wife. "I made up my mind not to be one of those picky mother-in-laws. I encouraged Luanne to redo their room any way they wanted. Well, about a month after they moved in I made a trip to Carmel for a couple of days. I paint and once in a while I like to go down and see the galleries. I take a canvas and do a seascape if the weather is good." When she returned she had a surprise waiting for her.

"On one side of the garage my dining-room table was standing on end and on the other side my sofa. The whole downstairs had been rearranged with things they moved in while I was gone. *Their* things. Mirrors, lamps, and photographs of mine had been wrapped and stored. I was days looking for everything. Well, I just sat down and burst into tears. And then I got angry. I don't know when I have been so angry."

Her son was surprised at her reaction. " 'It's no big deal, Mom!'—that's what he said. When I asked him how he'd feel if the situation were reversed, he said it wasn't the same thing."

She insists they were genuinely astonished when she told them they clearly needed a place of their own.

Carleton Hearst, a seventy-one-year-old retired insurance salesman, deplored his treatment at the hands of his physician. He described his annual medical checkup for which he has himself admitted to a hospital for a twenty-four-hour period. "The doctor comes in and says: 'Feeling a little tired, are you?' I say, 'No. I feel fine.' Then he asks me if my appetite is off. I say, 'I eat like a horse.' After a while he asks me what I do for exercise. I say, 'I walk a lot'—and I do. Maybe five miles a day. 'Is that all?' he says. 'Well, yes,' I say. 'Except for weightlifting and disco dancing.' He didn't think it was funny, but I don't care. If I had a pain I'd be afraid to mention it. I don't think I'd get out of the hospital. To that guy aging is a disease and he thinks I've got a full-blown infection."

In most nursing homes, minimal social considerations are thought not to apply to the old, and nurses and aides often come and go without the slightest regard for their privacy or feelings.

"I was standing there," Maude remembered, "completely nude beside my bed, while the nurse helped me into a fresh gown. All of a sudden in walks this fellow with a bucket and a big, long brush. The nurse walked off with my gown and helped him pull back the draperies. The window washer! All I could do was stand there and fumble about with a sheet to cover myself."

45

When it comes to social recognition the "Untouchables" of India have it better than America's aged. In a caste hierarchy that begins with Brahmin and Rajput, the Untouchable is at the bottom. Yet, though their tasks are lowly, they have prescribed duties and a place in the scheme of things. Ceremonially, economically, religiously, they are, as a group, indispensable to the full functioning of the village. Our aged, on the other hand, are literally outside a social system which seems to function *in spite* of their inhibiting presence. The old do not *like* it one bit, but a surprising number seem to feel, like the Untouchables, that that is simply the way the world is. They react predictably with a tighter grip on what does remain to them. If they build anything at all, it is higher walls. And with some reason. For society steadily usurps what they have left, eventually preempting even individual rights (regarded as invalidated by old age), rights to employment, to activity, to involvement with the passing parade, rights to recognition, to security, to sex, and to love. Even fate lends a hand as retirement, widowhood, and loss of close friends constrict further the character of one's personal world. So does sickness, and the general physical slowdown of age. The old person becomes hypersensitized to this attrition of resources, the acceleration of which he or she feels powerless to halt.

Destination "Nowhere"

What can the old do? What should they do? They have come to the borders of the social map as it exists today. Society designates no direction they can confidently move in with the sense of purpose and involvement with which they have moved through life until now. Since they cannot remain forever at a standstill and do not know how to move forward, the tendency is to backtrack a little—into known territory. That is why so many try to look younger. What they want is not so much youth itself. Even the very disturbed know this is beyond realization. What Miss Peabody and others like her want is the security which "less age" would provide. They want to get back on the social map.

"Sometimes, when I'm dressing," says Julia Arensberg, "I see behind my face to the face of my youth. The beautiful face. I put my hands at the temples and lift the skin. I cannot resist. A young face—a passport back to the *real* world, where things happen and people look at you as though they like you and want to know you, not run away from you."

While all change brings losses and some note of caution, the impetus that moves the young along is a positive, in many ways alluring one (though the loss of "youth" is not). Transition to adulthood brings new power, greater autonomy, a proliferation of roles, involvement as a decisive contributor to life. The move is upward. The shift to old-age status, on the other hand, is the antithesis of all these things. The move is unmistakably downward, and it seems no one is about to structure a route *to* it or *through* it.

But we need one—desperately.

Americans have established no procedures for leaving middle life with impunity or entering old age with cultural endorsement. I am speaking now of that amorphous, sometimes brutally turbulent period, when each of us comes to grips with an awesome phenomenon: the passing of middle age. It may last a day or five years. A few make a sick career of it. Each of us faces it with our particular personality, and from the perspective of our own personal world.

Men and women who review this period from a successful old age have shared certain basic attitudes and strategems. And they offer a compelling mandate for America's imminent old: the sole potential for success in aging in the United States today lies in full guerrilla warfare against the establishment. The old must fight for life and recognition and must be ready to do so on unconventional battlefields with all the psychic and social weapons they can muster.

In this second tactic of aging the initial step is clear: take stock. Take a long solid look at the personal world you have been building through the years. Then answer the question: is that personal world the best possible combat base you can make it? For confrontation with society, for the years ahead? For the out-and-out fight for *sanity* and *survival* after sixty?

"Anger helps a little," Hazel Arcero said. "Gets the adrenalin going." But free-flowing, undirected anger is fruitless. It is better channeled as a prelude to plans for action.

"I said to myself," Maude reported, "on your mark, get set, go! And hell, I went! *I was ready.*"

Those who make a success of old age do not do so haphazardly. They get ready for old age, stripping their individual worlds of the excess baggage, the outdated gingerbread of living that goes with outmoded roles and nonfunctional patterns of life. So many old live frightfully in sick museums of the past—like old Miss Havisham of *Great Expectations* who chose never to enter the present but made of her home and her life a relic of her youth. And it is the anachronistic accommodation of all these ploys that makes for a stale, clogged pattern of late life. Life without movement, forestalling the adventure of the present and the pull of the future.

"When my husband died, said Julia Arensberg, "it

was as though my life had ended too. How I mourned him! My life became just one long wake. Ours had always been a special marriage. I had fallen in love with him the first day I saw him, a young and handsome soldier, and we were lovers 'til he died."

She made of their room a kind of shrine, and for ten months she indulged a morbid preoccupation with the past, rarely leaving the house, seeing only her married son.

"I used to sit and just look at his pictures on the walls, I couldn't bring myself to part with his things. And there was a whole collection of Viennese waltzes that we used to play that reminded me of our youth before the war and my wonderful family. And I thought how they were gone now: my mother and my brothers and my handsome husband."

At her doctor's insistence she sold her home and moved in with her son, his wife, and their two small daughters. But it was to be a long painful time for all before Julia could discard her props, before she could make the first fragile gesture toward new life outside the stultifying prison she made of the past.

"It was a little thing, really, that triggered the change, the decision—whatever you want to call it. But it worked on me and worked on me. I was sitting in my room half listening to my granddaughters playing in the living room, when all of a sudden the voice of one of them dropped to the loud whisper of children. 'That's Grandma!' They were looking at the little picture of me on the bookcase, I thought. 'She looks different,' I heard Susan say. 'She looks . . . pretty.' And her sister, Tess, always the gentle one, said as though it explained everything: 'Well, she was happy then.' "

Julia looked at me. "The picture was two years old, taken when I was sixty-one."

She waited a moment and then went on. "I took a long look at myself in the mirror. I thought about my dreary looks and my dreary life in the house I had made so dismal. I thought about the past two years."

It took time to sort things out. She tried to put it into words. "I can't remember when I decided anything. There was a long period. A week, two weeks. I don't know that I even *thought*. Something seemed to hit bottom and begin a slow, slow rise. Little by little I was readier and readier. And then it was time. I sat down and wrote a letter to my sister in New York. I was going to change my life. I was going to make a trip. It was a beginning . . . and somehow it was an end. I knew it."

There is a kind of posture that must accompany this period of preparation for successful aging. Julia Arensberg sensed it, groped for it, and yielded slowly to its shaping. Not the ruminative self-hypnosis that gerontologists condescendingly associate with introspection among the old. But *a new adaptive stance*. The hopefulness for new things to come about and the will to help them happen, with a dextrous nudge if necessary.

It is good to remember the past, but the present puts an end to it, or should. "A man is really old," said John Barrymore, "when regrets take the place of dreams." Successful aging depends in fact on whether you remember the past as one part of life, or simply and wretchedly as the sum of life. Mr. Andromedas, a lonely, institutionalized Greek, betrayed his death-posture when, in reply to a question about work, he responded: "In my life, I was a waiter."

It is quite all right to assume this new adaptive perspective on aging even when it doesn't come naturally. As a matter of fact, that's the whole point of it. It is much like the formula ascribed by anthropologists to "imitative

50

magic"—by a staged acting out of what you want to happen, you set in motion the forces that actually *make* it happen.

The second tactic of aging, then, is the obligation to look around you as an old person, to get ready for the continuing challenge of life and for the particular battle the future holds for every person over sixty. The battle itself is another thing. But in preparation for it, every man and woman facing sixty (or already beyond it) must develop the strongest and most viable framework for action. This requires holding on to assets, compensating where possible for the losses that accrue with aging, and substituting new absorptions for the involvements now gone or inappropriate. Ultimately each man and woman must establish a new environment for living beyond the backdrop of middle life and the conventional world of work and family.

The major mechanism through which this is accomplished may be thought of in your overall strategy of aging as the replacement of lost satisfactions. It is the third tactic of aging. And it offers the most promising basis for full cultural incorporation.

The next chapter will be concerned with the dynamics of this task. It cannot be accomplished, however, without a surplus of hope over despair, of motivation over resignation. The knowledge that you must fight or let the world engulf you.

Tactic Three:
Replace Lost Satisfactions

"There were about fourteen of us," said Gina Rowles, who at sixty-four, in her first exposure to the diversions of the Golden Gate Golden Agers Club, found herself part of the crafts class. "We sat around a long table and apparently some of them were regulars. I took a chair and in a minute some woman came in and said I was sitting in her place, so I moved down to the end. There were two men off by themselves."

She paused, searching for the right words. "I had come because I was lonely. I wasn't at all sure what I wanted, but I had hoped to come away with the satisfaction of newfound company, of an afternoon free of loneliness."

She smiled. "I can laugh about it now, but let me tell you I never felt more a wretched discarded thing than I did sitting, like some mad character out of fiction, sewing together two pieces of bright felt. I've seen more engaging things in five-and-ten sewing kits for children. The director had a forced kind of heartiness. You had the feeling she didn't like us any better than we liked ourselves. A couple of women were really out of it and she spent most of her time saying cheery but rather impatient things to them. I couldn't think of a word to say to anyone. Most looked as unhappy as I felt."

Success in the struggle to be happy though old has surprisingly little to do with the physical assaults of late life. It has everything to do with the assaults of society. Old age, basically, is a fight for the continuing *capacity for happiness.* It is this the old must guard from dissolution or diminution. For the capacity for happiness is sustained in late life only by great vigilance and ingenuity: vigilance in making sure sources of satisfaction are maintained, and ingenuity in replenishing them.

A critical task for every man and woman who lives long enough is to find feasible interests, activities, and relationships that can be pursued successfully after sixty. These must replace the interests, activities, and relationships that were linked with middle life as these become inappropriate or nonexistent in old age. Meeting this personal charge is the critical third tactic of aging.

Making pot holders at some senior citizens' center just won't meet most people's need for happiness. It is a form of replacement all right, but not of the right order.

For replacement—or substitution—to work, it must involve alternatives of a scope comparable with the displaced satisfaction. We need activities and involvements that sustain and vivify a healthy image of the self.

The world about us is the only mirror we have of ourselves. We seek and need throughout life the continuing assurance of our identity. The absence of that assurance is emotionally crippling. When I asked a released mental patient what kind of person she was, today, at seventy, she shook her head. "I don't see anyone anymore to *know* what kind of person I am."

Some people seem to be born adapters and that is a

rich advantage in the post-sixty years. But the talent can also be learned. An invaluable, perhaps crucial, skill that appears highly developed among successful old people is the ability to *find* new areas of self-investment or, if necessary, to invent them. Related to this skill is the sheer insistence with which adaptive men and women demand of themselves openness to the advantages of aging, despite intermittent setbacks. Substitution will not work if it masks a manipulative last-ditch stand at regaining middle-age stature and middle-age roles. The subtlest self-deception here insures failure of the process. You can substitute for the pleasures and satisfactions of middle age but you can not *revive* them. Robert Marshall said it: "Once life is lived there are no refunds, and no returns."

It is not clear what drives adapters. But it has something to do with an instinct for survival, an almost animal drive to go on functioning with the species. It is a need to feel the aliveness, the social incorporation upon which personal identity itself depends. A confidence, not necessarily that one will win this struggle for life, but that there is no alternative to that struggle worth consideration.

There is in each of us an insistent and continuing need to feel our humanity. Through all our days we are propelled to see others, to be acknowledged by them, to act purposefully and freely. And in this we need to involve body and mind so as to know the cycle of stimulation, activity, and rest. Even into advanced old age.

Society frustrates these needs in her old members, severely muting them in many, but she never really succeeds in destroying them. In a way the adapters may be regarded as failures in society's planned dehumanizing program for its aged.

Adapters are practical. They work with what they have. Survival depends on it and they sense it. Facility in the area of substitution is fostered by a realistic view of life generally. The adapters do not expect all the rewards of life, but they do not agree that old age nullifies their rights to *any* of them. They are not without concern about their continuing usefulness. And if they are insecure financially, this can reach the proportions of nagging worry. Sickness is a constant foe. However, adapters see the issue of aging as one that confronts the best and the worst of us. It comes to all with the accretion of years. It needs resolution or compromise. But the ego is not insulted by the existence of the problem: it is never a question of personal unworthiness.

The problems of old age are basically the continuing problems of *life*, problems newly influenced by years added *to that life*—familiar concerns that revolve around health and wealth and self-realization, involvement with family and friends, the use of time, the need to love and be loved, sexuality, and the changing world.

One woman confessed to loneliness. "I miss having a man around, someone to look pretty and feminine for. I want someone to do things for, someone there at the beginning and end of a day, someone who cares. And you know, I hate sleeping alone." A man of sixty-two asked: "What do you do when there is no market for the only kind of work you have ever been involved in?" A widow confessed to such periods of depression that she sometimes felt suicidal. She had a very small income and lived far from her married daughter. Her days were long and empty and bleak with the limitation of poverty-level living.

None of these people was physically incapacitated, yet in their consultations with the very specialists charged with their assistance, a psychologist, social worker, and psychiatrist, respectively, the factor of advanced age precluded the most common considerations: She needs love. He needs personally to *do* something about his condition. She should be assisted in developing new interests and friends. In solving the problems of life—whether they related to kinship, sex, God, or work—advanced age, in the judgment of most Americans, obviates solutions that would otherwise seem mundane. It is an inhibiting and dangerous premise.

Substitution—Where It Starts

The main problem lies not with the experts but with older men and women themselves. Few have any perspective of their own lives. Few know how to *assess* the effect of time upon the familiar order of their worlds.

Old age is a chronic disrupter of conventional life styles. Retirement, in a work-oriented culture, is a classic disorganizer. It led Angelo the retired chauffeur to the brink of alcoholism and despair. Death of a spouse can be cataclysmic in a personal world which, like Julia Arensberg's, is narrowly focused on a mate. And a life patterned on competition and acquisition dissolves into a structureless limbo when we are moved out of the action. Often it takes a disheartening amount of time before we find the courage *and the direction* to move on. Miss Peabody, who knew nothing but the world of work, never did.

In the aging game, we need to develop the art of introspection. A concern and a capacity for it. We need to reflect on the daily *life* of life, to understand our own style of living and why we cling to it and how to adapt when substitutive changes are called for. And we need consciously to explore different, more appropriate life styles if a modified—or new—version is necessary to successful aging.

Most Americans have little training in this, and need some cue as to how and when to move along. Gina Rowles nearly succumbed to a psychotic depression when at sixty-one she was widowed through her husband's heart attack on a downtown street. Nine months later when I first talked with her, she had become almost obsessively concerned about growing old.

"I don't sleep nights. I lie there and worry over my life and what will become of me." A newly diagnosed hypertension distressed her.

"I am not to go up hills, and I have a habit of rushing up them, and that irritates me. What am I rushing for?"

For three decades her world had revolved around marriage and joint employment with her husband. Together they had managed an apartment building in a fashionable district. She was childless. Her most regular contacts were with a critical younger sister.

"It's true," Gina said, "I'm vegetating. I just sit and think morbid thoughts about myself. I didn't used to. I had my husband and we were busy. We had our little routine. But that's all gone now."

She constantly chided herself for minutes spent in late-morning sleep when she could be doing other things, but confessed she did not know what they might be. Lonely, she was fearful she could not much longer get around to do things. Her beauty operator told her she needed a boy friend and Gina agreed she did indeed. "But I should never have mentioned it to my sister. Now she thinks I'm some kind of sex fiend."

She seemed to be waiting for some magical change in her life, and a year later, when it had not come, her attitude was desperate.

"Here I am getting older, but I'm not going any-

57

where. I'm not doing anything. Something happens when you don't do anything. I used to work a crossword puzzle every day. Now I don't even read the paper. That's what worries me—losing interest. Or going downtown. It's like pulling teeth, and I don't like it. That's a terrible way to be. I think I could be like these elderly people who shut themselves in and never see anybody."

She was diagnosed as severely depressed. She seemed to sense herself losing ground irretrievably in a little understood but consuming struggle with society and with herself. "I can't make anyone understand. I want to *do* something but I just don't know what it is or how to go about it."

For many men and women marriage provides life's basic script—sometimes for decades. It supplies the cast of characters (spouse, children, relatives, even friends) through which they interact on a daily basis and achieve personal satisfaction and a sense of worth. For others it is work and the work context that set the stage. And this is particularly true for the generation born early in this century, who have known the calamity of the Depression and the almost unreal prosperity of World War II and the postwar years.

When we lose the marriage cast we lose the script and the cues for our entrances and exits, for activity itself. We love and miss the dead person, but also are left standing purposelessly in the wings. Retirement, then, takes us completely out of the action. We earnestly need direction. We need something special, something worthy and purposeful to fill the void. Men and women must make special adjustments—bring them about, force them—in a world whose familiar order has been changed, often significantly, by the passage of time.

Substitution—One Man's Approach

The key to substitutive skills lies in adapting familiar patterns of living to the pressures that age and society bring to bear upon them. Often the ideal strategy involves a combination of conventional and frankly innovative approaches.

Vincent Stewart figured out how. And he was to become a master strategist at the aging game. But the fact is that Vincent has simply continued to do what it has been natural for him to do for most of his life, but with new accommodations and with almost inventive flair.

Vincent was for thirty years a U.S. Marine. Over the years he came to adapt quite happily to an organizational framework which provides a ready-made set of coping mechanisms for the small and large adjustments that make up daily life. It furnished, too, the security which his early life with an invalid father had not.

The disadvantages were well offset by the sense of purpose, the ordered days, the certainty that his future, like his present, was ordained and governed. It was a part of the logical ordering of values that he was better off not to marry. "I'd seen too much unhappiness in the service among those who were married."

He moved widely around the world. "I learned to obey orders, and to give them and expect them to be obeyed. I learned that, under any circumstances, there is a way to get things done—a right way." The stamina he developed in the face of stress was to prove a permanent asset.

With retirement at fifty-six, Vincent decided he had earned a year's loafing. However, as inactivity loomed as a way of life, he realized he was making a mistake.

"You have to go on being what you are, and I had

never been a bum." After a try at sales work ("an unhappy experience") Vincent began "seriously to take stock of myself and my life."

"It was clear to me that I could not exist like this. *I was geared to a different style of life.*" He got a job driving with an armored car company. Within three years he worked himself up to a position of supervisor, directing a small group of men who drop off and pick up securities and cash.

At the age of sixty, he spoke candidly of his new life. We sat in his apartment and he watched with some amusement as I walked through the tidy rooms with him. The place shone.

"I don't empty ashtrays every ten minutes or plump up pillows when a guest stands, but I am what my girl friend calls 'almost pathologically neat.' " He opened a closet door and pointed to a low shelf of polished shoes, to the well-separated suits, and a storage area filled with labeled boxes.

"It's automatic for me. For *me*, you understand. Other people live in other ways, and in their places I never give it a thought. Mort, one of my closest friends on the job, is by the most generous standards a monumental slob. We balance out, I guess. And I can't help it any more than he can. Once I figured that out, I was a lot more comfortable with myself, and I don't apologize anymore for doing what comes naturally—not when it makes me happy and nobody miserable."

He and his comrades are close. Life is absorbing again after what he calls "a murky period." And, as a final gesture of adaptation, Vincent has abandoned attempts to cling to service ties. "Over time you find it doesn't work out. Old buddies move to other places or they die. I stopped going to the old haunts. And besides, I made new friends at work."

The shift in focus of his life provides familiar supports but with new elasticity, new corporateness. And in many ways the new synthesis is superior to the old. "In fact, I thoroughly enjoy the stable life here of going to work, falling into a good routine and making new friends. I think this is the first time in my life that I have really had a group of friends whom I see every day and can talk with on the same topics for some time. In the Corps you move around so much—too much."

Once again his close friends are the men he works with and his social life is a kind of extension of the job into leisure hours—parties, playing poker, watching sports events. The friends are retired from other jobs and most are married. Even in female companionship, the old group ties were influential.

"Woman I go with now had a husband who was an ex-marine. She's a widow and I've been going with her for the past three years. No marriage plans—been a bachelor too long, but we enjoy each other's company and we can talk about things familiar to us both."

He has insight into the continuing influence of the past on his present way of life. "I guess I still think like a marine. That has its advantages as far as I am concerned. I face life squarely now, just as I did then. In any case, I like to think I try." Retirement is seven years away, but he is busy now developing plans and financing for an intra-urban delivery service, specializing in perishable commodities.

Vincent could have vegetated and made a nuisance of himself, haranguing listeners with tales of gore and glory. He did not. Rather, he showed sensitivity and ingenuity, adapting to the disruption of a life pattern completely focused on a very limited source of satisfaction: group affiliation and its dividends.

When asked what the biggest change in his life was,

61

he said, "Going from military to civilian life." He does not automatically cast the problem of adaptation into an old-age one. For Vincent, as for the old everywhere, *advanced age is not the cataclysm*. Rather, the problem is one of adaptation to changes that accrue with the dissolution of a pattern whose coherence and satisfaction-quotient are dependent on a vanished status.

"It is hard to come really and truly to recognize that you can't remain as you were, that you're not in the service anymore, and that you have to face a new kind of life. The old system doesn't exist anymore. That's the gist of it. It's just not there, like it once was there. Now you have to find a new one and this is hard after too many years in the old routine."

This awareness of the inevitability of change prepared Vincent, after an initial false start, for the work of adaptation. The decisions he made were not random. Rather, they constituted logical compromises, a way of extending to best advantage the fruits of years of living. He was alert for opportunities to ease the stress of transition and to terminate features that had no promise.

"On the van I worked out all right. There were experienced men who were retired like myself and I realized I fit in nicely. Still, you know, civilians don't talk the same language as professional servicemen. Even communication was different, for it takes time to learn the new language. Also, you have to develop new interests, so you can talk to people when you meet them."

The scope of his world has been reduced, but he considers the related changes to have been triumphs of accomplishments, not testimonies of defeat. This perspective, *one he says he taught himself*, is a rich advantage psychically. It feeds, rather than corrupts, his sense of worth, his humanity. Age is only one of many relevant variables in the business of living. He regards his continuous adaptation to age and a more restricted daily schedule as extensions of valued strategies, not as surrender to a shriveling life space. He has purposely shaped a new life around familiar rewards of sound relations with his fellow men. And it has paid off. He has *made* it pay off.

The patterns against which Vincent structures his life as an old person operate with no less impact in all our lives. Generally, however, it takes digging to make them discernible, even—perhaps especially—to ourselves.

It took Constance Cramer one year to make the substitutions that brought new order and new meaning to her world as an old person.

"I had the worst Christmas of my life," she told me. "Every carol was about as joyful as a dirge. I promised myself that, come the next December 25, life would be different."

She missed a house full of people. "You can't raise six kids and adapt very readily to Christmas in an empty house. I was in my element with kids around. One year we didn't take the tree down until Washington's Birthday. It was eleven feet tall and when I bought it the man thought it was for the lobby of some building! The house was full of laughter and I loved it."

She showed me photographs of her husband and her children. "Every year they'd have a group picture taken for me. It was the best gift of all as far as I was concerned." With her finger she circled a blond boy who sat with his hand in his father's. "That's Toby, the youngest. He was born when I was forty. He died of muscular dystrophy when he was twelve, and after that none of us had the heart for a family portrait. I nursed him through those final months. The doctors said he would never have lasted as long as he did without the care he had."

When, ten years later, Constance's husband was killed in an automobile accident, she found herself alone in the large, four-bedroom house.

"The kids are gone. Three of them live out of the state now and they're all busy with their own families. Every single one of them has asked me to come and live with them, but I really can't imagine not having my own place—and I love my house. Fortunately my husband left me moderately well off financially."

The phone rang. "That will be Ellen, my oldest," she said, moving into the hall. "If she doesn't hear from me by 11:00 A.M. I usually get a call."

When she returned it was with coffee and cookies on a tray. In a few minutes she put down her glass and resumed her story. Her New Year's resolution, she said, was to find something to do with herself. She began her search with the want ads.

"Somehow I never thought of volunteer work. I think that would have helped me find myself a lot sooner." Each morning she would spread out the paper and read every help-wanted entry. "I learned more about what I couldn't do than what I could, but it set me thinking."

She went to several employment agencies but was appalled at her reception. "I filled out forms tirelessly. There were always a few key questions that were designed to make you feel like an idiot. And if the forms didn't, the interviewers generally would. I was never sent out on *anything*. You have to have a skin like an armadillo."

But she did not give up. "It was clear to me that advertised jobs went to younger, college-trained people with experience. I wouldn't have wanted most of them anyway."

She hesitated, trying to reconstruct her thinking. "I knew I was good with kids. But I couldn't teach and I didn't want to babysit. I went to half a dozen little preschool nurseries but they had waiting lists."

One day she met a friend of hers for lunch. "'I think you're out of your mind,' she said. 'With a home like yours I'd be trying to stay in it, not get out of it.' Well, I just stared at her. It had never occurred to me to look for something to do in my own home. I was so excited I could scarcely finish my lunch."

After that, Constance said it was a matter of detective work and stamina. "I talked with everyone I knew. I called the children long distance and asked them to come up with ideas. The library has all kinds of books on starting businesses and I read anything that seemed remotely feasible. At one point catering appealed to me, but I didn't like the sales aspect of it."

Then, one morning, Constance had a call from her daughter. "She asked if she could borrow my foldaway cot for the weekend. She was going to take care of a neighbor's little girl whose brother had fractured his leg in one of those ugly skateboard accidents. They were bringing the boy home from the hospital that afternoon and she figured the parents could use the time to get him settled. 'I don't know what they'll do on Monday,' she said. 'The mother teaches third grade and the father's in law school. And that poor little kid will be home for a month. What a mess!'"

That was in March. "In April my son's twins went in for tonsillectomies at the same time. He took a week's vacation time when they came home. They weren't all that sick but it was still impossible for Joan with the two of them."

However, it wasn't until May that something happened and, for Constance, "the pieces all fell together and I was clear in my mind about what I wanted to do."

She went to a luncheon and fashion show sponsored by one of the local hospitals to raise money for a new playroom in the children's wing. After the lunch there was an open house at the hospital. "I was amazed to find so many 'sick' children playing house, throwing bean bags, and even riding around on tricycles.

" 'It's a familiar syndrome,' one of the nurses told me. 'Too sick for school but not sick enough to be in bed all day. Most of them still need special care, and it isn't every home that can handle them.'

"That was Saturday and on Monday I called my doctor and told him I needed to see him for a few minutes. He must be almost my age and he's been taking care of all of us for twenty years. It was he who diagnosed Toby's muscular dystrophy. I can't bear the thought of his ever retiring but he says not to worry—he intends to die with his stethoscope on. I sat in his waiting room until his last patient left and then I told him what I was thinking about. He didn't tell me I was too old, or that I'd wear myself out, or that I was being foolish. He said it was a brilliant idea and someone should have thought of it sooner. 'A kind of convalescent home for kids! It's a crying need.'

"He encouraged me to see how I'd relate to sick kids, to give it a try. Then I went to see an attorney and he told me what I could and couldn't do and said that when I was ready he'd draw up some papers for parents to sign for my protection.

"I spent hours walking around my house, imagining it with children again. I confess that at that point I wasn't at all sure what to do next."

But Constance had set in motion the forces that would decide the future for her. About three weeks after her visit to him, Dr. Byrne phoned. "He told me to stock up on Jell-O and brush up on my lullabies. 'We'll start you off with an easy one,' he said. 'The girl is nine. Her name is Madeleine. She contracted measles her first day at summer camp and they're shipping her back. Her mother called me in a panic. There are three younger kids and she's not had any of them vaccinated.' Before I could think of what to say, he added: 'The bus arrives in two hours. And, Constance, they haven't a relative in the state.' "

Madeleine was the first. Mrs. Cramer put her in the yellow bedroom, next to hers. "Whatever reservations I had about my abilities were dispelled in no time at all. They say once you learn to swim you never forget. Well, I think it's the same with taking care of sick kids."

That was eighteen months ago. Between Dr. Byrne, word of mouth advertising, and concerned school and hospital groups, Constance could have every room in her house filled. But she hasn't.

"Three is an ideal number. For them and for me. They entertain one another." For Mrs. Cramer the house has come alive again. Loneliness vanished. And once a year the additional income pays for a travel vacation she could not otherwise afford.

Her life has changed in other ways. Two nights a week a young nurse relieves her. "On Tuesday I have a seminar at the university on the hospitalized child. It's fascinating and I've made some new friends." Sunday afternoon is "a kind of open house. It's a chance for parents to get together and talk. They realize they're not the only ones in the world with a sick child and they feel better."

She has resisted opportunities for a full-fledged commercial operation with larger quarters.

"I like my life exactly the way it is. Once again I have people who need me and whose lives I can make a little easier. The tempo is right and I am better off financially than I have ever been."

Last December I received a card from Constance—a photograph of her, surrounded by ten of "her children," and an invitation to come and toast "one of the happiest Christmases ever."

Few men and women have come to realize as Vincent Stewart and Constance Cramer have that, in late life, new roads to satisfaction find their surest direction from established junctures. Therefore, few search them out as purposefully as they did. Few think to build upon that life style to which they are geared in thought and action, and through which they have learned to find everyday sources of emotional and social satisfaction.

Substitution: How? With What?

Knowing what age strips from the individual is sometimes valuable but more often simply obvious. One may be no longer spouse and lover and companion, or cook and nurse, chauffeur and confidant: vanished roles peel off lives like leaves from an artichoke. This kind of focus is not on what remains, on the heart, but on the discards, on what was consumed and is gone. It fails to confront the jackpot question: what is continuing, salvageable, reconstructible? This needs to be the primary focus and the base for substitution. Even unhappiness in those who have suffered severe loss can be relieved by developing remaining relationships or finding new ones. The process by which this is accomplished emerges as of critical importance, perhaps universally, for the old in pointing the way to social and psychological resilience in late life.

Not everyone seeks as diligently as Vincent Stewart or Constance Cramer to reconstitute the same formula for living. Some find new satisfactions by making prominent in their lives what had been secondary skills or interests. One man made of a lifelong interest in woodcarving a profitable part-time avocation. Another who had a passion for fishing, which he could never fully indulge as family head and wage earner, put a down payment on a boat which he rented out to fishermen in Baja California when he was not out in it himself. In two years it was paid for. Today he works as little or as much as he wants. A woman pigeon fancier taught herself ornithology and opened a small bird hospital in her home. In two years she was successfully marketing a special bird feeder by mail. Of great satisfaction to her is the friendship of neighborhood children who bring ailing wild birds to her. She has constructed a large outdoor aviary. Prior to her retirement she had been for forty years a corset saleswoman.

For these and other men and women, the end of marriage or of the work role provided both the time and impetus to activate interests better suited to their late-life circumstances. Seemingly new involvements were actually latent patterns of satisfaction, muted formerly by insistent role demands of adulthood and middle age. Men and women who succeeded in developing a different and happy equation with society often demonstrated unusual ego strength. Unlike Gina Rowles, they were not unnerved by society's instructions for exiting. They simply and unobtrusively returned to the scene by another door.

In some ways it is our eccentrics, our life-long eccentrics, who slip most easily into a trauma-free old age. Least touched by the strictures of American society, they are made least distraught by release from them.

Men and women of her age group, says Delia Adams, grew up in a period of rich potential for the cultivation of eccentricities. Delia, who at sixty-three enrolled in her first sailing class and two years later sailed alone with her newspaperman husband to Hawaii, found life "really very different" when she was a girl in San Francisco. "You grew up in neighborhoods—we really don't have neighborhoods anymore. You lived much more intimately with the people around you and somehow it was important to assert your individuality and respect it in others."

She was, she thought, much like her mother. "We were both movie buffs, but we followed the careers of movie stars and gangsters with equal interest. We lived vicariously through the wild adventures reported about them. They were all heroes and heroines to us. I remember my mother used to say that John Dillinger was welcome for dinner any day of the week. Used to drive my father crazy."

A secret poetess, Delia published a volume of love sonnets, and at twenty achieved instant notoriety and a financial windfall. "The poems were inspired by the popularity of *The Sheik*, an old silent movie my mother used to talk about. I called the book *Moroccan Nights* and signed it with some Arabian name I found in an encyclopedia. I never dreamed it would be published. It was the kind of thing that wives hid in their lingerie drawers and high school students read in the rear booths of coffee shops after school—full of panting kisses and pounding blood. It would be thoroughly comic if released today."

Her father, she recalled, "had a fit and I moved out into an apartment of my own. Unmarried girls of nice families didn't do that in those days, and my aunt said it was clear that no self-respecting young man would ever have me." She shook her head, remembering. "Actually I was thrilled to be on my own. I've never regretted what I've done. Any of it."

We were talking in the tastefully furnished apartment she shares with her husband. Delia rose, went to the mantel, and returned with a photograph of him that she said was taken when he was forty. She smiled.

"He has always been content to let me be me. And you know, he says if I wasn't born a renegade I sure took to the role fast enough." Replacing the photograph, she spread her arms out, palms lifted, "Just lucky, I guess."

Like Delia Adams, most of today's eccentric old developed early in life a distinctive and actually age-free living style. Having thumbed their noses long ago at our hallowed values, they are not, as old people, concerned *for the first time* with substituting for them. They crossed *that* bridge a long time ago. Accustomed to living on the fringes of the social map, they may now feel extraordinarily at home with the ostracisms of age.

Some are the product of lifestyles that shaped a relatively isolated existence. In our survey these men and women generally enjoyed few close friends. Some had inordinately narrow interests which they pursued alone: a self-professed animal trainer who developed a little cat and bird act which he performed for clubs, a woman who spent her days on the piers logging the ships in and out of San Francisco harbor, a proselytiz-

71

ing socialist who delivered the party newspaper in the
Tenderloin district. Most of these men and women had
fled or failed in marriage early in their lives and were
long-time loners.

The Creation of New Life Patterns after Sixty

Most old people, however, do not begin as experienced loners. They are, whether they know it or not, in
search of a pattern for living. Middle age ends and with
it familiar patterns of action lose applicability, and no
new links to life are automatically served up by the
culture. None. No formulae for the satisfactions and
challenges that made life worth living. Distraught and
confused by the change from positions of social mean-
ingfulness and security to the amorphous loneliness of
age, they don't know "how to get there from here"—
how to meet this problem that grows and torments and
somehow lacks the kind of definition that permits one
really to grapple with it. They don't know what they
need or want or how to get it. They don't know how to
frame the problem.

Yet one must learn to think and act *as* a problem-
solver to win at this aging game. Men and women who
survive society's treatment of them as old learn to
phrase and face problems with calculation. They choose
"strategy" in terms of their given environment. And
where problems defy traditional patterns of solution,
they seek, or invent, new solutions. It is a faculty critical
to successful aging. And it can be learned.

Whether layman or scientist, each of us acts by apply-
ing to a given situation or problem the set of rules, the
code of behavior, *the pattern of coping* that has in the
past been applied in similar situations or problems,
which is fine and time-saving and commonplace. It

works in the majority of cases. But the rub comes when we face a situation in which traditional patterns of action are ineffective. They just won't work.

Arthur Koestler uses "matrix" to designate the total number of moves possible within a formula for action. But, as he points out in a discussion of his theory of bisociation, "however flexible the matrix may be there comes a point at which it sticks. The scientist then finds himself in a situation comparable to that of Gambetta in 1870 when he wanted to reach the provinces, and was hemmed in by the Prussians surrounding Paris. All possible exits were barred, so what could he do? He made his escape by balloon. Gambetta's balloon corresponds to the different matrix, the different set of rules, that the scientist suddenly discovers, and thanks to which he escapes from the blind alley."

Blind alleys take many forms and so does escape from them. What is distinctive of Koestler's combatant and my "aging adapter" is not the urge to get out of the trap they are in. In the face of stress and its tensions the drive for relief is common to all of us. What is unique to these individuals is a sense of problem, a compulsion to find their way out by creating (in the absence of alternatives) their own solution to the situation that entraps them.

Scientists create by virtue of their unwillingness to regard a problem without a solution as an *insoluble* problem. Aging adapters create for the same reason basically. They will not agree that old age is the terminus of life that society assures them it is. Both opt to do something. To consider anything. However, theirs are not irrational attempts at action. Both draw upon all the knowledge of past performance from their own and others' experiences. Both dare, if not consciously, then as a kind of intuitive stance, to think in terms of discovery, that is, to assume that the present situation will yield to manipulation. Of course, a critical part of any solution is the initial statement of problem. Gambetta would have been buried in that field by Prussian invaders if he had restricted the problem to conventional tactics. How then could he ever have thought of going *up?* But he *had* to go up to get out. Or down. Some way other than the conventional ways which were irrevocably closed to him.

In considering the increasing numbers of men and women over sixty for whom it has no use, society has labeled the problem one of "old age." And the old themselves accept this phrasing of it. But old age, as such, is not amenable to resolution—unless you think of eventual death as one. Old age is not reversible. You simply have to live long enough.

"I'm old," Maude said. "I'm old! What in the world am I supposed to do about that? But my daughter looks at me as though it were some travesty I persist in. Nurses are often the same way. After a while they get petulant with old people, as though we're trying to put something over on them. As though we could— what?—be younger if we really cared?"

If "old age" *is* the problem of the post-sixty population, it is unresolvable. And some gerontologists, I am sure, hold to this. These are the minds that espouse through a gagging array of rationalizations "storage" facilities for America's old—as a resolution of "the problem of their presence," as one researcher phrased it. The problem has been cast into one of care of the old, of coping with our obligations in the face of this mounting burden. Resolution then centers around whether there should be a few large centers or many local ones, if these should be urban or rural, professionally staffed, linked with hospital facilities, offering therapy, with wards or small rooms, self-regulated or staff-directed. No one really bothers to go back to the premise that set this whole storage fiasco in motion. Why storage? Why not incorporation and usefulness so long as that is possible? And it is. It *is*—often even for the sick and the disturbed. If we would only *seriously* consider the how of it.

The problem needs to be recast. What we need to ask is *not* what we can do about the running out of life, but what we can do about this continuation, this extension of life. We need to be life- not age-oriented. To what use can life be put after sixty? That should be the direction of our concern. Within this context we can begin the actual phrasing of questions that will themselves point the search for answers. Is the problem really one of having something to *do?* Something to *be?* Or is this dichotomy of our making? Is it artificial and distortive of what should actually be all of a piece, a way of life, a way of being *and* doing? We need to put the individual back into aging, whole and entire, concerned with life as he or she has lived it and as he or she will continue to meet its challenges.

Where existing life styles cannot accommodate the changes that late life brings, they must be adapted, substituting new satisfactions for vanished ones. Bold, free experimenting in innovative patterns will enrich our late years and change them from social burden to cultural asset.

When Helen Kagan, a widow on reduced income, couldn't find a decent apartment at reasonable rent she followed up a different kind of ad. "Three college girls were advertising for a fourth to share their furnished house. They didn't know what to make of me when I appeared bright and early on the doorstep. I think they were just in shock when they agreed to give it a try," she said, laughing. "But it has worked out so beautifully that they have asked me if I know of someone who would be right for three of their girl friends who have a place out near San Francisco State. I pay $100 a month rent, and since I started fixing dinner for us, why they won't let me contribute to the food budget. I have my own room, and when the girls feel like it they come in and chat, or show me a new skirt, or borrow a needle. They keep what hours they like and so do I. It's lively. I like it."

Kitty Haines told me that all her life she'd been "a night person" struggling to get up in the morning. At sixty she decided to do something about it. She quit her job with an insurance company with full pension and took a 4:00 P.M. to midnight shift at a busy all-night donut shop. When I met her a year later she was learning the baking end of the business and excited about her new pattern of living. "I talk to people from all walks of life. Most of them are regulars. The truck drivers taught me CB talk and I got so excited I'm working for my ham radio license in my spare time—which I've lots of. Get to bed pretty much the same time I used to, and I'm up at 8:30 or 9:00 A.M. with the whole day ahead of me. I love the luxury of late breakfast and the morning paper."

Gourmet cook Dennis Wylie missed the adventure of the kitchen after his wife died and his grown sons moved away. He combed the neighborhood, talking to friends and strangers, and volunteered to prepare party food for them at cost in their kitchen or his. "I specialize in hors d'oeuvres for groups of six to twelve," he told me, "but lately I've been branching out. I volunteer to help serve at the larger parties, and I'm busy almost every Saturday night. It's great entertainment. One guest invited me up to his weekend place. We fished and I cooked the catch!"

From the time he saw his first play at the old Alcazar Theater, Christopher Blake had entered into a permanent love affair with the theater—something he thought he might get into "if only I had the time." At fifty-eight he decided to take the time and volunteered his services to a number of small Bay Area repertory groups. A good-looking man with a hint of a British accent, he eventually was taken on by a small group and in nine months progressed from ticket-taker and set-mover to bit parts. "Surprisingly, there just aren't that many older people around ready to put the effort into little theater work," he told me. An English teacher, he continues his high school job but hopes to devote full time to the stage when he retires in four years. "By then I should have the experience for it." He says his students look upon him with new interest and that he wrote his first play last year for the senior dramatic class. "I feel marvelous," he confessed. "But why the hell did I wait so long?"

Malcolm Payot returned to school at fifty-seven. "Decided to go to law school. Always wanted to be a lawyer. What the heck. Couldn't have lived on my pension anyway. Borrowed money to pay the tuition and for a used car to go to school." He passed the Bar "a week before my sixtieth birthday." He has a job with a state agency and specializes in discriminatory hiring and firing cases. "In seven years, when retirement here is mandatory, maybe I'll plead my own case." He gave me a slow wink. "Or, maybe by then I'll be ready for something else."

For Mavis Riordan the world of art came vibrantly alive when she invested seven dollars in the rental of a watercolor of an unidentified landscape from a local gallery. It was the first painting she had ever acquired, and her interest in determining the locale led her into the study and eventually the cataloging of regional landscapes in California. Today several galleries use her system as a research resource and her work brings her in contact with many artists. She is invited to numerous gallery shows. "I'm really not in it for the money," she told me. "I don't make that much at it. But it's exciting. And I meet fabulous people." Aesthetic satisfaction is not the prerogative of the wealthy. Especially not where the rich heritage of our cities is accessible to all.

Where challenges seemingly defy solution we need to remind ourselves of our basic malleability and of the range of social adaptations possible to us in the United States if we will only consider them. And until society does consider them, the old *must* do so by developing specific strategies for personal fulfillment and for cultural survival.

It is the fourth tactic of successful aging.

Tactic Four: Develop the Resources That Count

MONEY AND WORK

It isn't always easy. Maria Ortega knew. Her son, Pedro, had needed money, rather considerable money,

78

and he had come to her—confident in her love and largesse. For Maria at sixty-three it was to become a time of peril and of liberation.

Exactly how much money she had, Pedro did not know. But he knew that she had a bank account. To have virtually quit work meant that she had the security of some reserve. And hadn't she always placed her sons' welfare before her own? It was her heritage. Part of being Mexican, of being a woman, and of being a mother.

It had taken ten years of accepting infidelity and brutality before she decided to take her two sons and leave her husband. She had entered the United States as a field hand, and they lived on starches and in the cast-off clothes of the families with whom she found domestic work when the children reached school age. She saw what life had brought to the families around her, and made up her mind that her sons would share in it too.

As the boys grew older she encouraged their self-possession and deferred to their judgment. Pedro was her pride and joy. He went to college, found a good job, and eventually married Kathy, whose stenographic job ended with her pregnancy.

And now he was standing in the doorway of her small apartment. Alone. He had come without his wife. He had come on a mission. The last two weeks, Maria knew, had been a strategic buildup. Two invitations to their home for dinner. A ride on Sunday. She had not been allowed to help in the kitchen, and Kathy had not frowned when she forgot to call her son Peter as his wife preferred. Kathy, a bright, lovely woman who at twenty-three spoke with an assurance that was still alien to Maria at sixty-three.

Now Pedro stepped into the small flat. The living room always came as something of a surprise after the bleak communal staircase. Maria herself had decorated it, the very first place of her own. Today it was especially inviting and serene with its soft yellow walls, the polished floor that reflected the warm Mission District sun, and everywhere the evidence of her patient handiwork. The small throw rugs, the chairs she had bought secondhand and re-covered (at night school), and the curtains that had taken weeks to crochet, for they were made of a thread so delicate that when the wind blew through the open window it seemed to send into flight a half-dozen fat, winged cherubs that formed the border design.

The flat had amazed Kathy, who had heard of but never seen an antimacassar. She was intrigued by the way they clung, despite their heavy starch, to the arms and backs of the chairs. Her mother-in-law's home, she said, gave her an odd feeling almost of vertigo, as though she had crossed some enormous chasm of time.

Pedro and his wife were furnishing a modern redwood home in Briarwood Heights, just south of the city, with a beautiful view of the Bay. They had gone heavily into debt to acquire the down payment and now were hard pressed to furnish it. And there was a baby coming.

"How about a beer?" Maria said. They were both more comfortable in the kitchen, and he liked the old wooden table with the round bins that slid away from the side, filled with flour on one side and sugar on the other.

"How's Kathy?"

"She's okay, Ma. She's fine."

They talked about little things. She was waiting for the overture. Waiting. Dreading it, but somehow hoping it would come and be over. She knew what she had to do. And then, "Her birthday's next week."

"Ah!"

He pushed his long legs under the table and then pulled them out again. With the beer glass he etched a wet circle on the oilclothed table.

"Ma, there's just one thing she wants. That she's got her heart set on."

She didn't help him. But he was almost there. And she could very nearly read his thoughts: this gesture would give her pleasure. Hadn't she always wanted his comfort and happiness? He would see to it that she lost no interest on her money, and at the same time he would avoid the large commercial rates that were draining his resources. He was already heavily committed. And, of course, he would be as conscientious in returning it as he was with his other obligations. And he was there, if she *should* need anything. Even in the unlikely case of a slightly prolonged delay in the repayment of the loan, he could envisage no great inconvenience to her.

It came out nevertheless more baldly than he had intended. "She'd be the happiest woman in the world, if she could just get that wall-to-wall carpeting we need. There's a special on, one month only. All wool, Ma. That's the best. With bare floors—everything could get scratched up."

The words kept coming. He wanted her to know that her money was going to be well spent. That was the hard part for him, making sure she understood that her money would go to a good cause. He understood her deep-rooted respect for moving slowly, for thinking things through, for patience. They had done this thinking for her, Kathy and he. But, curiously, she had failed to sense where he was heading, what he was waiting for her to say. To offer to do.

"You understand, Mama. This is a hard time for us."

The briefest pause. "If we had just a thousand dollars—before the sale is over. Now, while we can get it."

Later on, when Maria thought about it, when she talked about it, it was the calmness she remembered.

"I could see my life, like down a dark tunnel. And I was at the door looking out at the light. I could not risk going back, not down that dark way again. At twenty you can do it. I did. At twenty, *they* can do it. And they must. I helped him get ready as best I could. He is as ready as he will ever be."

But she could not tell him all those things.

"I said, 'No, Pedro. No.' Just that."

When Pedro finally left it was not in anger, but Maria could see that things would not be the same between them for a while.

"But that is all right," she said. "We love one another, but there are things that I am learning, that he must learn."

For Maria Ortega the encounter was a kind of test, and though she could not readily dispel the anguish she felt for her son's plight, she had emerged from their meeting more confident in her own future. This somehow neutralized the pain and left her with an odd mixture of exhilaration and pride.

It is a posture not easily acquired by the bulk of older Americans. The present older generation of women is largely alien to the women's liberation movement and the joyful cultivation of independence. Most feel out of character spending money on themselves, and some men and women experience acute guilt if they do not remain bountiful parents even to middle-aged children.

One of the most difficult things to learn in late life is *not* to trust your most generous instincts. Mother love is great—Americans revel in the imagery—but not if it does mother in. Looking out for yourself as a priority concern is something that you must learn to do—with aplomb, pleasure, and good humor. Those who don't learn may have another lesson in store for them, the rueful consequences of dependence, which is the only alternative to independence.

The enjoyment of late life calls for more calculated strategy than does any other life period, but that circumstance in itself presents no insurmountable obstacles. Strategies can be broken down to specific ingredients, almost like recipes, once the goal is specific. The only elusive variable has been the commitment of the old.

But once that is a fact, once aging is accepted (Tactic 1), a readiness stance assumed (Tactic 2), and one's capacity for continuing satisfaction protected (Tactic 3), the confrontation itself provides its own stimulus. At this point the task of the old person is to use all amassable resources—material, physical, and psychic—strategically to get on with the business of living, to operationalize old age (Tactic 4). It is the jackpot task. It is the validation of one's option for *life* itself.

Anything that will maintain or improve access to our culture's mainstream needs zealously to be conserved by the post-sixty American. Where possible, resources should be expanded, but these opportunities are often limited. Under no circumstances are resources (tactical advantages) to be yielded. Particularly, older Americans must hold on to wealth, health, and all those assets that help them to resist efforts to alienate them from life. These include, importantly, their access to love and sexuality.

Even where assets are extremely limited it is a mistake to give, loan, or confer power over them to others. It is unwise to be dependent on the counsel of sons, daughters, brothers and sisters, or well-meaning friends. Although these people may be well-intentioned, they are often too involved themselves to divorce the welfare of the older person entirely from its implications for their own future.

Like the gentleman who went up in the balloon to escape an enemy, the aging individual must learn to view the total context of the problem at hand, analyzing resources, and then act—as the situation demands for survival. More lives have gone needlessly down the drain of time through fear and inertia than have ever been lost through injudicious or innovative moves. There is always a way out of the strictures of late life, especially when one learns to read the signs of approaching threat. With a little practice older Americans can become master strategists of their success. They must.

What I want to discuss here is the strategy involved in maintaining and expanding the advantages that have greatest tactical value in developing a satisfactory style of life—though old and though American. Dealing successfully with family, friends, and strangers is a part of the strategy of aging and will be dealt with in detail in later chapters. But before one can talk about with whom and in what direction to move and adapt, a more immediate challenge must be met: With what? What do you need to *have* to age successfully? What assets count?

There is nothing mysterious about the conditions that facilitate successful aging. I remember speaking with a panel of consultants charged with evaluating our aging research. What, they asked, is most critical to keeping America's old out of mental hospitals? When I responded with "wealth, health, and love" the panel members made it clear that they regarded such a conclusion a poor return on a costly research investment. I don't see why. It was valuable to confirm with 1,200 men and women what had always been obvious to all but the scientific community.

Wealth

No individual can abdicate responsibility to anticipate basic needs as an old person and to develop early those strategies that will insure those needs are met. It is folly to speak of lifestyles and aging adaptation to men and women who are immobilized, literally, by poverty. It's like asking a woman clinging by her nails to a mountain ledge what plans she is formulating for the future. You cannot age successfully without money, some money, unless the life of the hermit or hobo is one to which you have made previous adaptation. Indeed, even lifelong escapees of this type run the constant risk that their aberrant lifestyles will be interpreted *in old age* not as the privilege of eccentricity, but as evidence of senility, and they will be institutionalized.

The possession of wealth is a master value of American society. The conspicuous consumption of it occupies too much of adult living as we work simultaneously to spend and save it, never acquiring enough to do either as effectively as we would like. Inflation and taxes now dissipate our most heroic efforts. A simple twenty-four hours of breathing seem to incur a fantastic outlay of cash, and the satisfaction of "needs" has become a life-consuming burden for most of us. And it

85

gets worse for the older American. It is part of society's prescription of slow death for which the old have yet no antidote.

In the United States today, the old have half the income of the under-sixty-five population. The national average is $296 a month as compared with $586 for the rest of Americans. Three and a half million older Americans, or one in seven, live *below* the official poverty threshold of $2,720.

The poorest of the poor in the United States today are the older women. Fifty per cent live in poverty. Especially disadvantaged are black females, for whom the incidence of poverty reaches the astonishing proportion of three out of every four.

Older Americans are not only poorer than the rest of the population, but they are embedded more steadfastly in poverty than any other segment of it—Blacks and Chicanos and American Indians included. Even where the income of older persons has shown some increase (largely because of fitful improvements in retirement payments), the rise has not been as rapid as for younger groups. Economic problems dominate all developments in aging, with even modest consumer needs beyond the reach of most persons past sixty-five.

Rachel Mooney, a seventy-year-old retired garment inspector, receives social security payments of $173.00 a month. Eighty-five dollars goes to the rental of her one-room apartment, and with a budget of less than $90.00 she must meet all other expenses. She eats meat once a week, cajoling the butcher sometimes for extra scraps for a nonexistent dog.

George Jackson, a former linotyper, has a $150.00 monthly pension, plus a regular $30.00 dividend from an insurance policy. He is so closely budgeted that he has not seen a movie in two years or had a new article of clothing in more than four. His main source of diversion is an old television set he picked up in a flea market. It works without sound.

Helen and Seth Mackay had to sell their car because they couldn't afford its upkeep, but increasingly they can't afford public transportation either. They live six urban blocks from the nearest store, ten from church, and a mile from the park where Seth likes to read and discuss politics with a small group of habitues. As compared with their $3,480 annual income, the retired-couple budget prepared by the Bureau of Labor Statistics for a modest but adequate intermediate standard of living came to $6,738 in autumn 1976. A lower floor-level budget came to $4,695.

The present post-sixty generation of Americans is the product of circumstances that are strategically devastating in the struggle for economic, and hence social, upgrading. The older the individual the lower the mean educational level. Almost half never completed elementary school. Only 6 per cent are college graduates. The Depression was responsible for aborting the educational ambitions of many whose meager resources would not cover the expense of books, transportation, or sometimes adequate clothes.

Rick Karner, who did get himself through college, recalled that he would sometimes alternate with his brother the use of one pair of "good shoes."

"I worked for my uncle in a little tailor shop on Mason Street, and I struggled along with night classes at the University of San Francisco. Took me six years to get through. Actually we had it better than a lot of people but there was a stretch of about two years when things were really tight. I got shabbier and shabbier. My brother used to work for O'Connor Moffatt—where Macy's now stands. He could buy his clothes almost at cost. I convinced him to lend me his shoes when he got home at night and I'd wear them to class. They were a little big but that didn't bother me. Everybody used to pool clothing in those days."

Rick had always wanted to be a lawyer, "but I figured I was lucky enough to get as far as I did."

Although generally savings-oriented, the average older American was never able to acquire enough reserves to come even close to insuring a trouble-free old age. Those who were able to put money away or to buy a house sometimes found their economic picture adversely affected by it. In a bureaucratized welfare society, many became ineligible for assistance in times of economic crisis. Many saw the products of a lifetime of effort dribbled away in a single catastrophe.

Henry Alexander went through $18,000 in savings—profits from thirty years as a furniture maker —as a result of the double illness of his wife and himself when both were in their mid-fifties. At fifty-seven, in relatively good health again, he was unemployable in his old trade because of a slightly stiff right hand. With no idea what else to do, devastated by the slow attrition of resources, he moved from frustration to depression and in five years was psychiatrically confined, his wife on welfare.

Even in good health the old find themselves in desperate straits. Small raises in rent, penny increases in staple foods, an interruption in even the smallest contribution from a son or daughter, a hole in a shoe, create crises. By the most appalling economies they fight and withstand loss of independence to the point often of virtual self-obliteration. Widows who see their limited savings vanish and must abandon homes and possessions of a lifetime for small housekeeping rooms. Old men living in flophouses. Surviving couples who take care of one another, foregoing basic medications to go on eating. The men and women in their "good clothes" who sun themselves on park benches and hate the bleak, rainy days when there is not even this escape from their changeless rooms. The very old scissors grinder who survives on sixty dollars a month and discarded supermarket vegetables, living in a lean-to of his own construction, fearful of discovery and confinement. "Old Kate" who collapsed from malnutrition and wept three months later when she was discharged from a state home, where for the first time in five years she had three meals a day. "I don't want to stay here," she said, "but I am afraid not to eat." The janitor who takes care of his ailing wife in the basement room of the building he services. Sick or well, they see institutionalization as the end of identity—and they are right.

In such cases the economic decimation of the old attests to their social condition, *not* their potential. The confusion of the two, however, projects an image of America's present-day old as an intellectually limited, educationally stunted group of low social promise—an assessment with which society is basically comfortable. Devaluation of our aged is easier when they are viewed not as a disadvantaged group but as an inferior one. Children of the old San Franciscans we studied sometimes went to ingenious lengths to mask this "inferiority" of their parents—reporting usually more formal education for their parents than the parents themselves claimed. These seemed quite content to view themselves as self-made men and women. And they were. But it is by cultural consensus not enough, even retrospectively.

The older population is not the homogeneous and static group most Americans think it to be. Further, the 5,000 "newcomers" who every day in the United States celebrate their sixty-fifth birthdays are quite different from those already sixty-five-plus. They are cultural worlds apart from the "very old" born around the turn of the century. Their expectations, educational backgrounds, cultural horizons, and basic creature-comfort needs will establish a very, very different threshold for successful aging.

The condition of the old is not only a wretched one, but a dangerous one as well. Dangerous for the living potential of those now old and for all who will one day reach sixty-five, or nine out of ten people alive today in the United States. The "fact" of poverty among the elderly establishes a precedent for a group without precedents. And we love and cling to precedents. We run the grave risk of accepting substandard existence as another component of old age as inevitable as wrinkles. We are, I think more than halfway there. The Special Committee on Aging of the United States Senate warns that "a new class of elderly poor is in the making among those now fifty-five to fifty-nine."

Old and poor is par for the end of contemporary life. The "old" is unavoidable; the "poor" should not be. There is little likelihood, however, that significant change in the plight of the old will come about until they themselves *do* something about building adequate reserves, insuring their right to work, and structuring retirement years to their advantage.

Building Reserves

"I have lived too close to poverty not to remember the chill of it," said Eva Manigore. She had fled Nazi Germany in the late 1930s and worked for two years in New Jersey, making artificial flowers until she learned enough English and saved enough money to open a small hat shop.

"Financial advice is not hard to get—and it's free. I asked, asked, asked, and I learned how to take care of myself and plan. Even when things were very tough I would make myself look ahead. And now I have a little income—every month a check, not much but enough so that I am free."

That, she says, is "a big thing. How else could I have walked out of my son's home, made a trip, and today do those things that make life worth living—a movie, a concert, tea sometimes in a nice place. And once in a while something pretty and new."

A continuing and adequate income, however, is rare. More feasible perhaps are convertible assets through which to earn money, or to become involved with life in a way that doesn't require sizable resources.

"I used to work in a bookstore on Sutter Street," John Fox said. "When I was sixty-five they retired me on an income of a little over a hundred a month. I had a little reserve but not enough for the rest of my life, though I certainly didn't think I'd see eighty."

Besides, inactivity riled him. "I'm as lazy as the next one, but it's too much of a good thing. I have a salesman's mentality, I guess. Mainly I love the stimulation of meeting people, getting to know faces, pushing a good product, developing friends who come back again and again. Time flies. You *feel* good.

"I live just off Kearny Street. And I used to walk down in the morning and buy my paper. Up and out. Had to go three blocks. And one day it occurred to me. I was in a kind of in-between zone, midway between the Broadway strip and the financial district. *Just* the spot for a newsstand."

He paused and smiled broadly. "I've been there fifteen, almost sixteen years now. I'm eighty-one. Feel great. When the new office building went up, they built a matching stall for 'Foxy'—what do you think of that! I've even got a heater and a one-plate burner for soup."

Survival is the rawest but most critical measure of the resources of an individual—or a culture. And most of us expect more out of life than mere survival. But in the aging game, that is a chancy premise. It is the unexamined expectation that reasonable needs for food, shelter, security, and human intercourse will be met that causes the adult American to be duped in the aging game. More men and women need to anticipate the insidious shift in ground rules that makes basic survival a guarantee at forty and a privilege at sixty-five. They need to anticipate it early if they are to face late life with the greatest tactical edge.

The Right to Work

Today only one in three Americans over the age of sixty-five is a part of the work force, with concentrations in the lowest-earnings categories: part-time work, agriculture and self-employment. Overwhelmingly, the majority are, de facto, denied *any* opportunity to make money. The one-half to two-thirds cut in income which is routinely experienced at retirement cannot be replaced.

Yet, despite the striking success of federal legislation outlawing the practice, the pressure for earlier retirement and decreased employment opportunities after sixty-five is being intensified in many sectors and deliberately cultivated by unions. It is estimated that within five years—if the present trend is allowed to

92

continue—80 per cent of Americans aged sixty-five and over will be entirely outside the labor force.

Formulas that adjust retirement payments for inflationary hikes are of meager assistance since, at best, they provide only for restoration of the previously inadequate living standard. Further, they offer "catch-up" assistance—*after* economic disaster—forcing depletion of any savings the old may agonizingly attempt to maintain. And inflation is ever on the increase, adversely affecting whatever purchasing power retirees do have.

Since 1965, the total health bill alone for the aged in the United States has more than tripled, including (importantly) the costs of medications and institutional care. For example, in the last twenty-five years the cost of a hospital room has catapulted from $15.00 to $176.00 per day. All of us suffer from this, but the burden of health costs is monstrously oppressive on fixed incomes. Cost sharing under Medicare continues to increase, and monthly the gap widens between items and services covered by Medicare and Medicaid and those which must be paid out-of-pocket by the older American. Once the old are on the economic treadmill to social oblivion the task of reversing the process is awesome.

Unless it can be shown that mass incompetence infiltrates the working ranks of American men and women on the eve of their sixty-fifth (or seventieth or seventy-fifth) birthdays, the policy of calculated economic incapacitation should be identified for what it is: the retrieval of economic resources from a devalued segment of the population for the benefit of a more valued group, the young. For despite federal legislation attacking mandatory retirement practices, the convictions that determine who will work and who will not in the

United States today remain essentially unaltered. The older American is set apart from the rest of society and classified as a non-productive member.

The same aggressive pressure that is forcing long overdue changes in the work picture of Blacks and Mexican Americans must be brought to bear by the older American. Discrimination is just as powerful and inhibiting on the basis of age as on the basis of color or sex. Retiring a man when he is sixty-five *because* he is sixty-five involves the same kind of prejudice as not hiring him at thirty because he is Black. In neither case is the basic issue of ability to contribute constructively examined.

Our rigid pattern of sustained work through middle age and unrelieved retirement throughout old age provides a poor base (psychically as well as financially) for successful aging. Yet Americans as a nation are caught up still, despite some innovative challenges, in the sacred character of work. Work *counts*. We can think of little else that does *count*. Even the dulling atomization of work counts in a technologically-driven universe.

If work is sacred, retirement is profane. Gerontological literature and consumer magazines, too, are rampant with dolorous warnings about it. And when retirement does come, early or late, most are nervously steeled for it. Yet, while a minority, like Amy Peabody, face a kind of psychic disfigurement with retirement, the majority are not reluctant to be relieved of some of the strictures of work.

Carl Pincoski chose to retire earlier then he had to, "while I was still young enough to enjoy outdoor living and to boost my retirement income with a new job."

He made careful preparations for a proposed geographic move, spending weekends roaming through the redwood forest area of Humboldt County, an area he loves. "I'd go into small towns off the beaten track. I'd keep my eye out for local newspapers. Then I'd read them through—social activities, coming events, and especially the ads. You get a darn good idea what goes on in a place, what property costs, what the jobs and businesses are. I'd talk to people in coffee shops and in gas stations. You get a feel for the place. I'd spend my weekends that way. Sometimes I'd go back to the same place two or three times. See it in spring but see it in winter too."

Carl enjoyed the search and at the end of fourteen months had worked out an appealing package. "I got a great little house, a stone's throw from Scotia. Only ten years old, huge stone fireplace, and I took over a mortgage that will cost me less per month than I've been paying in rent in San Francisco. That area is developing like crazy. Figure I can always move the house." Two afternoons a week he has a job with a lumber mill, guiding visitors through the facilities—a job he got through the newspaper. He leased the last available shop in a new artists' compound five miles from his home and used his woodworking skills to sell custom-made frames, trays, mirrors, and—his specialty—fine wood dressers.

"My costs are low. I have virtually no overhead." And he enjoys the stimulation of contact with people who like nice things, with his young neighbors "who watch over me." The sign over his shop reads "Pincoski's Refuge."

Structuring Retirement

For the old generally, retirement is not stressful. Even when included in a checklist of problems, "retirement" was dramatically slighted by our group of old San Franciscans. *It is what comes with retirement* that is stressful. And the distinction is meaningful for the aged and for their fight for successful aging. For Angelo it was losing identity, having structureless days and nothing to take pride in, facing the end of the social incorporation that went with *work* incorporation—these were stressful.

In the new workless universe that society has shaped for its old, few have learned to compensate for the personal satisfaction, the social vitality, the success gauge that work provides, largely because society is woefully remiss in serving up alternatives.

Retirement can become desirable only if it offers the promise of a culturally endorsed "non-work" period for all Americans. The closest we have come to this is a costly substitute. We have become nervous consumers of leisure, structuring our retirement time as we did our work time, extending the Protestant ethic to a demanding fun-and-games syndrome. And this is very expensive business. Only a fragment of America's old population can afford the socially defensible retreat of "leisure towns" and the conspicuous consumption of leisure as a full-time pursuit. A great many would not, in any case, choose to accept, even if they could, this escape from what is the real challenge: something worthwhile for them to do with their lives beyond the work-glory-money syndrome. It is basically not an issue restricted to late life.

We are just now seeing the first, bright signs of new directions: patterns for a longer, more flexible, better balanced, differently integrated life, and a view of life that embraces both work and non-work in new dynamic interactions. Perhaps one such pattern will be school, work, retirement in middle years with time for personal and social investment in community-action programs, environmental exploration, and travel. Then work, perhaps school again, and intermittent periods for recuperation and insight. The old line that has traditionally been drawn between work and retirement will shift and diminish to the great advantage of the old, if they prove adaptable enough.

Some firms are working to change things, but they are too few and the pace is turtle-slow. The push must be for more individually tailored retirement policies that take fairly into account individual differences in ability, stamina, and continuing promise. Widespread experimentation is needed. Its goal should be the better adjustment of individual needs to economic mandates. Among possible innovations are: broader use of sabbatical leaves long before retirement age to retool older employees, to allow them revitalizing experiences of study and travel; trial retirement where company and old person experiment in getting along without one another, with salary adjustment in a transitional period where retirement needs and living style are established; and part-time work for the same company in later years. Pools of consultants and troubleshooters could be formed of skilled old people by factories, manufacturers, business firms, and educational institutions at the time of retirement. On-the-job training could be initiated for the gradual development of secondary careers, and the invention of new employment for older persons encouraged, particularly in areas of pressing social need. The federally supported Foster Grandparent Program was such an invention, and now men and women from more than forty states and Puerto Rico earn much-needed dollars as they bring warm one-to-one loving care to lonely and institutionalized children.

Our government, local and federal, could do much more to assume a position of leadership in retirement planning. That it does not, says William Mitchell, who for years served in an advisory capacity to the American Association of Retired Persons, is in large measure a result of the absence of pressure from the old themselves "because of their lack of awareness as to what *could* be done." An apathetic top business management throughout the country, and the low social priority of the subject of old age generally, compound the plight of retiring Americans. Although one in three of our unemployed are over forty-five years of age, only 10 per cent of federal funds budgeted for retraining goes to this group.

We have the knowledge and can, if we care enough, call on the resources and talents necessary for the continuing education or re-education of every post-sixty American. Men and women who have been phased out of areas of declining interest—milliners, owners of small neighborhood shops, traditional craftsmen—could learn new applications of basic skills or develop new careers. Refresher training programs could teach mechanics the use of new tools, typists how to use electronic machines, and teachers new approaches and new markets for knowledge. Those whose employability as bus drivers, manual workers, or in demanding sales work is threatened by waning physical resources could take up less taxing work. Widows looking for work—some for the first time—could be rescued from unemployment or menial labor.

Any older person might explore a wide choice of arts and crafts. And by this I mean the development of quality work, not just artsy-craftsy diversion. The New England Arts and Crafts Program, which has endured since the Depression, is an excellent example of the tremendous possibilities of support in just this one area of learning. A product of efforts to utilize indigenous materials and designs to raise living standards, the pro-

gram trains people and obtains for them enough re-
muneration to supplement, meaningfully, income in
retirement. This project is not restricted to retirees,
but they are heavily involved in it.

Successful aging is a matter of stance, of learned
perspective. And it is a matter of learning to "think
old"—whether one is twenty or forty or sixty—and
build all possible assets as a bulwark against future
problems, especially to insure flexibility in the shifting
lifestyles that may come with old age.

Money is important. So is some kind of work or pro-
fession or role that involves us with life and engenders
purpose and direction in the passage of time. The significance of these assets cannot be overemphasized. But
they *can* be stripped from us. Despite our canniest precautions. What cannot be stripped is a readiness to take
advantage of new opportunities, to monitor alternate
routes to critical resources if these routes become necessary. Practice in this monitoring should be an absorption. A satisfying one. As automatic as careful driving.

In our acceptance of late life, we must accept too the
opportunity to make of retirement a period of personal
and social growth. We must also demand that society
provide the minimal resources to bring this about. If we
do not, help will come only in dribs and drabs in the
familiar too-little and too-late pattern that perpetuates
poverty for every ninth American.

PHYSICAL AND MENTAL HEALTH

Physical Health

We are "grown-up," it seems, for a long, long changeless time, and then, imperceptibly at first but with

gradual conviction, we and our bodies are older. Into some days there intrude strange pockets of fatigue. The sense of buoyancy and bright surges of sheer animal energy come less often. Small but nagging discomforts invade our peace of mind. Little aches, muscles that throb now when they never used to. Dentists grow fussier about mouth care and make absurd and non-apologetic references to receding gums. The thermostat becomes difficult to read. And most threatening of all is the full-length mirror. Somehow even one's best, one's party-gala best, doesn't project the same old dash. In movies and books one finds oneself identifying, not with the slender nameless ingénue but with character actors, movie greats, many of them—though a surprising number of quite grown men and women have never heard of them. Even the handsomest are now jowly and wrinkled, transformed by bodily changes from which even they are not immune. And with an eerie empathy, one reads of the passing of men and women little older than oneself.

Time leaves evidence of its passage upon our bodies as upon our lives, again inviting dangerous concentration upon what has been lost to us (what *was*) rather than upon what remains (what *is*). Sound health and a firm body are devoutly to be wished and worked for and protected, but the absence of robust health is not synonymous with disease or a rationale for the end of active involvement with life.

Health is a diffuse concept; its meaning is relative to some scale or standard. The word carries connotations of "best" or "optimum"—terms difficult to define. Americans are enormously health-oriented, obsessively so, by cross-cultural standards. In a half-starved world, the average United States citizen (well-fed, well-clothed, and well-housed) frets about tired blood, vitamin-deficient meals, pink toothbrush, and "ho-hum mouth." Happiness U.S.-style presupposes radiant well-being; there is something *wrong* with the person who doesn't radiate. He is a candidate for some kind of therapy. We regard glowing health as the normal, natural state of things, and disease as a departure from our normal condition. The sick person is by definition abnormal. For the majority of the world's population the converse is true. In the United States, the below-par individual is suspect and, as our television commercials suggest, a social liability. The implication is that we can stay healthy if we want to. By such logic, disease becomes a willful perversion; the sick person, a social deviant.

Health is to be flaunted culturally in the hectic, blatant activities of the young; in the savage confrontations of organized spectator sports wherein only powerful, conditioned bodies can go the distance and take the punishment; in the flawless physiognomy of movie queens and heroes; and in our distinctive patterns of leisure (amusing and confounding to so many foreigners in our midst), which often are more physically demanding than our work. We insure ourselves against disease. And the 1970s saw the rapid development of comprehensive health programs with growing emphasis on preventive medicine, validating, on a national scale, every American's right to bountiful well-being.

In the United States today neither poverty nor old age can be an excuse for failure to keep up with cultural standards, however unnatural these may be. Our socially cultivated fantasies of optimal health levels for all who care enough and work hard enough to reach them doom the old (and the very poor) to failure. From time to time the implied culpability of the old for their physical state is dramatized in the media.

"Would you believe this woman is fifty-five?" runs an ad in a popular magazine. And the exercise, foods, and "attitude toward life" that presumably made the svelte blonde what she is today ("at the peak of attractiveness") are awaiting every reader. The masses learn that health and stamina are indeed the birthright of worthy Americans, any worthy American; witness the still-dancing stars of the 1930s: Fred Astaire and Ann Miller, long-legged, effervescent, and glowing with life. But the credits are not associated with a well-lived long life. Instead these idols are awarded the greatest of compliments: they are "perennially young."

The most damaging effect of our stance regarding health is not the abusiveness heaped on the *natural* symptoms of physical aging. It is rather in the aplomb with which Americans lump into a single category— old—the moribund, the highly deteriorated, and the sick (4 per cent of the post-sixty-five population) together with the one in nine Americans who is simply over sixty-five and predictably not as young as he or she used to be.

Four in a hundred post-sixty Americans are physically beyond anything but the most superficial social interaction. But 96 per cent are *not*. They are ready for it, need it, can meet it more than halfway. It all depends upon what you choose to emphasize. To see. And to acknowledge.

No sixty-year-old will run the mile in record-threatening time. But the majority can legitimately disdain the wheelchair for a time yet. A disquieting number of seventy- and eighty-year-olds are far from it.

Among those we interviewed were fourteen daily joggers, ten who swim the year around (two in the cold waters of San Francisco Bay), twenty bowlers, eight tennis buffs, and a veritable strong man who was offended by a question about his health and promptly lifted an oak dining table into the air with one hand—after he got the interviewer to sit on it.

Predictably, sickness and impairment do have greater impact upon the post-sixty-five age group than upon any other age segment of our population. No one denies that. They are comparatively less hearty, more vulnerable to injury, and have the greatest incidence of physical and mental illness. The National Health Survey reveals that four out of every five persons aged sixty-five and over have one or more chronic conditions. Before we translate this statistic into a rationale for shelving the old (as is customary), let's look at the data from a more positive perspective. What these figures say is that the majority of old people live with disease or impairment of some kind. What they fail to say is that this is a problem common to Americans regardless of age.

Chronic diseases affect almost half of our total population and more than seven out of ten persons aged forty-five and over. Of the approximately 87,000,000 Americans of all age groups with one or more chronic conditions, 22,600,000, or more than one-fourth, report some degree of activity limitation. Furthermore, while the old are sicker, the greatest increase in age-based rate of impairment is in two areas: impaired vision and impaired hearing, both of which are more susceptible to treatment or correction than, say, arthritis, rheumatism, or high blood pressure, which are only negligibly higher among the old than among the 55- to 65-year-old age group.

Mental Health

About one of every four persons admitted *for the first time* to a public hospital for the mentally ill is sixty-five or over. This is two and a half times that of the younger population. Why? Have they become more perishable mentally? Our findings in the study of 600 psychiatrically confined old San Franciscans did not support such an interpretation.

There are more old people in mental institutions today in large part because there are more old people than ever before, and because they are the fastest growing segment of our population. Improved health resources, such as Medicare and Medicaid, although insufficient to the needs of the elderly, also allow readier identification of all disorders than was previously the case. But more old people are in mental institutions because our culture has become more efficient in putting them there and more dedicated to keeping them there.

The population exodus from rural to urban areas has hurt the aged, both the migrating old and those who grew old in cities. Old people are not absorbed into our cities in ways protective of their physical and mental health. Like any minority group, they find their strengths vitiated by poor physical and social environments, often by actual slum conditions.

Louisa, "the witch of Jones Street," moved to San Francisco from the Napa Valley when her fifty-year-old son was fired from his agricultural job and found work in the stockroom of a large San Francisco wine company. They lived in a two-room flat on one of the city's steepest hills.

When asked what was the most stressful thing she ever had to face, Louisa replied unhesitatingly: "The confinement. The way we lived those last years. It was bad when there was no work in the valley, but somehow life was better. I was out in my garden all the day. The city is no place, not when you have to live like that. I tried to stay cheerful because it was hard for my son when he saw me unhappy."

It was the neighborhood children who gave her the nickname "the witch of Jones Street," and a host of fantasies built up about this woman who sat through the day, at the window, almost toothless in a peaked black knit cap (which encouraged the legend that she was bald). People were mildly afraid of her, and on her infrequent sorties up and down the stairs-like sidewalk, avoided her. When she smiled at them anyway, she confirmed the consensus that she was senile.

At seventy-eight, when she was committed to a mental hospital, eight months after her son's death in an automobile accident, she tested "in robust mental health" and was transferred to a state home for the aged.

Where new trends in urban planning such as the Model Cities Program have resulted in changed environments for the elderly, the incidence of their hospitalization for mental *or* physical illness has declined. Mental illness among the old seems more firmly linked with broad civic problems relating to their social incorporation than with age-linked deficiencies. The higher admission rate for treatment of mental illness reflects more a problem in housing than one of mental impairment. The rest of the population is more likely to have someone to turn to and less need for largely custodial care. According to the National Institute of Mental Health the *outpatient* psychiatric clinics in the United States serve more persons in the ten to nineteen age group *than in any other decade of life.* One-fourth of all clinic patients are adolescents. And this does not include the large number of students receiving college and university psychiatric and non-psychiatric counseling services. If the present trend continues during the next decade, although the total number of resident patients in mental institutions will decrease by 18 per cent there will be a further increase of almost 90 per cent in the rate at which young people are institutionalized. These figures do *not* include narcotic admissions, 50 per cent of which involve youths between fifteen and twenty-four years of age.

The old categorically have health problems, but so have the young. So have we all. But proper treatment, hope and love, and social accommodation can restore many of the even chronically disturbed elderly to home and community. We are training more specialists in geriatrics and fewer of them are accepting platitudes about the irreversibility of disease among the old. We know more about the nature of these diseases. We can do more surgically, removing, repairing, or replacing inadequate organs. We can do more with drugs. And psychiatrists who once figured the life expectancy of the old did not warrant their consideration as long-term patients are seeing the training curricula of medical schools revised to incorporate new therapies for the old. One physician, who joked with me about a new field of gerontological obstetrics, had attended his first fifty-four-year-old mother.

Performance

There is no doubt that response, motivation, and general performance levels change with age. Flexibility, physical and mental, tends especially to diminish with *inactivity*. If there is any demonstrable finding of experimental studies in aging, it is the trend toward a decline in psychomotor skills with age. But in none of these areas is the trend unrelieved or decisive. An experiment at Cambridge University involved a group of persons from fourteen to sixty years of age who were asked to throw links of chain at a target, then over a bar in front of the target, and finally to aim it at the target through a mirror that reversed the near-far dimensions of the target. Only in the mirror test did the oldest subjects fall behind the youngest. The assumption on the part of psychologists was that the mirror test called for a fresh organization of incoming stimuli.

With progressive loss of stimulus input with age, the organism tends to become less "keyed up," or set to respond. Social factors are potently influential. We conspire to remove the old from *sources* of stimulation: from work and social activity and human involvement. Thus their tendency toward cautiousness or inflexibility in certain tasks may not reflect a generically anxious or uncertain disposition, but rather a defensible bid for more information, more involvement.

A further distortion of the condition of the aged is a product of the research design of most projects concerned with comparing them with younger age groups. Experiments are designed, as one researcher put it, "to test crucial qualities." Crucial for whom? Crucial for what? Testing is for the most part designed to show the degenerative effects of aging and feeds a shocking tautology: the tendency to interpret what older people can do by what they are asked to do. The bulk of their potential never invades the research arena or violates the limited or distortive format inherent in the basic research design.

What do we test? Speed and timing, performance, productivity and achievement, motivation, and motor skills. What would you anticipate in the way of results if you pitted forty-year-olds against twelve-year-olds in a contest of jacks and hopscotch? Would you direly document the adults' relatively poor performance, their lack of coordination and of the motor skills critical to success, and then draw conclusions as to the obvious correlations between this and their continuing social usefulness? Forty-year-olds are quite legitimately no longer physically involved in the same way at the tasks they did at twelve. Nor are they as an age group characterized by the earlier, more broadly adaptive skills. In the assessment of their performance level, the comparative evaluation, while accurate, is irrelevant. It suggests failure in a context that distorts the very meaning of the term. Further, the adults have skills deriving from superior strength, greater size, and broader experience that are *not* being evaluated under the existing testing conditions. And many skills are highly complicated processes that are difficult for the most highly trained psychologist or physiologist to localize. There are no simple generalizations in the identification of age-limiting factors.

The assets we look for in our old are those that are most valued and at their peak in earlier life periods, during youth, adulthood, or middle age. Why do we find it so significant to demonstrate their lesser appropriateness in old age? Why are we not just as assiduously seeking to identify those assets that *are* old-age linked? They exist. The trouble is their identification depends in large measure upon what side of the entry sheet you are registering them. Caution is negatively translated by most experimenters. This is because speed is more positively valued in most of the observable test situations. But caution where alternatives are suspect is commendable. We drive fast and faster and the relatively slower driver is said to impede the "normal" flow of traffic. That this normalcy results in more deaths a year than the total loss of life from cancer and heart conditions combined has not affected the premise that speed counts, or influenced the accommodation of slower drivers on our nation's highways.

According to the National Safety Council, on the basis of a survey of 3,500 old drivers and statistics of 200,000 accidents involving drivers of *all* ages: "Age is neither the best nor the only indicator of fitness to drive in modern traffic." It simply produces a different pattern of accident from that common (and hence more acceptable?) to the American norm of fast, aggressive driving.

In assessing performance of any kind, great emphasis is placed by behavioral and social scientists on motivation. One researcher defines it as "the intensity or frequency of the individual's exposing himself to the learning experience." High scores on motivation testing are equated with the ability to modify behavior, a highly valued trait in our change-oriented culture and a *necessary* one for the old if they are to make the adaptation to age with success. But is the "learning experience" as accessible to the old as to the young in American culture? The theory of disengagement, the widely endorsed approach to successful aging, is built on the desirability of removing the old from continuing social involvement. It makes the *reduction* of motivation normative for our old, a state which researchers then deplore as evidence of their reduced performance level.

For the post-sixty American *there is no basis extant for positive physical and psychic evaluation.* Any kind of assessment, other than a dire report of damages, of what aging may contribute, remains fantasy. The truth is that nobody *knows* what the old can do or what they would be further capable of if supported and encouraged.

109

And the most short-sighted group is that of the professional specialists in aging who sell their subject short. When the old patient recovers from a serious illness the physician generally considers him abnormally resilient, saved by wonder drugs, or simply perverse. When a mentally ill patient is judged well enough for release and return to community life, the psychiatrists congratulate one another, never the patient, except in the most platitudinous bedside manner. The old are viewed as commodities to be *acted upon*, intrinsically incapable of self-launched activities. In this way, people are made to lose identity.

While all patients, regardless of age, face something of this depersonalization, it reaches an extreme with the old. It is as though they were not *real* people. As though they had gone over some ledge into an abyss beyond meaningful incorporation into social life. When they live in submissive dignity, despite a poverty-level existence worse than that which forces our Blacks into revolt, they offend by their suffering. And we exert all social pressure to limit their mobility and autonomy at a time they most need it, intensifying their isolation.

Strategically, the old are in as much a bind physically as they are financially. They can't win. Or, more accurately, society would prefer that they did not win and has stacked the deck, merging the well and the moribund in one "sick" category. In a way, the undermining of their physical and mental resources is more insidious than their economic decimation. The label "poor" is an accurate one. "Sick" is not, though it (more than the former) has been applied relentlessly to the old in justification of shelving and ostracizing them.

Sick and old have no inevitable correlation, and such an assumption should be resisted actively. The older

Americans must guard especially against the temptation to believe it themselves. Theirs is the obligation to take care of themselves, not to accept marginal health as their physical or cultural due. Theirs is the challenge to work for better standards of preventive medicine, insurance coverage for regular physical checkups the prompt treatment of reversible ailments, and active good health. They have a mandate to stay active, to remain on and with the scene.

In a thousand small ways the old can repair a ruinous social image of themselves as inevitably sickly. The use of pseudo ill-health as an attention-getter may pay off in short-term responses, but talking sick, or thinking sick, or indulging preoccupation with inevitable body changes makes for morbid company. When chronic disease requires attention, accelerated health care can compensate greatly in the prolongation of active life. And finally, even in the face of progressive and pervasive health problems, there is only compounded agony in the abdication of one's prerogative to *life*.

Cy Hart made a profound impression on all of our interviewers. Alert, intelligent, serene, and wise, his self-acceptance is complete. Crippled with disease, forced to wear a urinal at all times, and nearly blind, Mr. Hart—first interviewed at ninety years of age— gave us his philosophy of life. "I have an original motto which I follow. All things respond to the call of rejoicing; all things gather where life is a song."

At ninety-one his physical condition no longer permitted him to indulge in his hobby of wood-working, and now at ninety-three his failing eyesight rules out television and limits his reading to one hour a day. Yet he takes his declining physical functioning in stride, and insists it is not irksome to make the necessary adjustments. He finds it somewhat "humiliating" that he

111

has outlived three wives and both his sons, but his mental faculties have remained remarkably intact. He is proud of this, attributing it to the philosophical orientation he has worked out for himself and incorporated into his life. Such a philosophy has strategically nullified age's most sustained physical assaults.

LOVE AND SEXUALITY

Luther Shaw's lady friend, he told me, describes herself as "homely as hell and tough as beefsteak." They met at the baseball park. Both are avid fans and attend games with such regularity that they came to know one another by sight, though they had never spoken until the day Lucille joined a stampede down the aisle to catch a home-run ball.

"She's little. I thought she was going to get killed in the rush," Luther said. "And I just found myself on my feet running protective interference." He shook his head and laughed. "She needed about as much help as a rampaging bear. The kids didn't have a chance. And when she raised the ball triumphantly overhead the crowd applauded."

His face kept the broad smile, but his voice was sober and even when he added: "We were friends from the moment we spoke—and lovers soon after. I love that old witch."

When I commented that he made her sound less than lovable, he was briefly silent, studying me with a look of frank disappointment.

" 'Lovable!' What's 'lovable?' A pretty face and a pretty disposition to match? That's a combination that bored me at twenty, and I'm sure not looking for that at sixty. Lucille excites me. And that's the truth. I like the laughter in her face, the quickness of her movements, and her supple body. I like her wit, her spunk, and her love of life. I love the way she draws me out of myself— the teasing that lets me know she cares."

He hesitated. "I'm not sure she was ever 'pretty.' But it's a face I'll be happy to look at for the rest of my life. I'm just grateful to have found her."

Luther and Lucille chose not to marry, and live apart largely because Lucille takes care of a chronically ill sister and is reluctant either to leave her or to bring Luther into the restrictive home life imposed by her sister's condition. Both she and Luther bear with good grace and obvious amusement his son's displeasure over their relationship.

"He called us decadent," Luther told me. "And when I relayed the comment to Lucille she said to tell him she was insulted—she wasn't decadent, she was liberated, as liberated as he was. Oh boy, he really got upset because he figured I had let her know about *his* girl friend. And he was right. So I said to him, 'The less said about your sex life or mine the better. Okay?' Lucille and I laughed like hell."

The kind of pleasure that Luther and Lucille have found in each other is something that many older men and women would also like to realize. However, most are hampered by two convictions: first, that they are physically unlovable, and second, that loving— particularly making love—would be judged shameful by their families and friends. Lucille and Luther discounted the first, and were blithely disdainful of the second.

In the aging game, men and women who avoid or ignore opportunities to love and to be loved create absurd obstacles for themselves. Tactically they vitiate emotional resources. They surrender the incalculable advantage of emotional exchange, the power of basic human affection.

The Need for Love

Many of the so-called chronic diseases of the old are essentially testimonials to the chronic absence of loving contacts. And this includes the opportunity for involvement with close, caring friends.

A Greek waiter who ran away from a state hospital despite the cautions of physicians and staff that he could not live a month "on the outside," was interviewed two years later:

"Another week," said Apostolos Andromedas, "and I *would* have been dead. I told them if I'm gonna die I want to do it with my friends, where it matters. But I didn't tell anyone how sick I was. Damnedest thing. Makes you wonder about those sawbones. I took the medicine they gave me till it was gone. I ate whatever I liked, mostly Greek stuff you don't get in those places with all their boiled mush and baked cardboard. When I got out I weighed ninety-four pounds. Would you believe it? My shoulders stuck out like meat hooks. That was December. Had Christmas with the gang. By March, I weighed 120. April I got my job back and I ain't been back to the doctor since. Would take an army to get me back."

The old who are without human affection deteriorate. Those in state homes and in convalescent hospitals develop ways, well known to every nursing aide, of compensating for the absence of love. There is the ceaseless attention-seeker whose call light is always on, and always ignored. This person wants water, a bedpan, a pain pill, a pillow straightened, the bed lowered (or elevated), to know if a meal is ready (or to tell you a tray should be returned), or to find out if a daughter or son has phoned, or where the newspaper has gone— endlessly. If he is up, he wants help in getting to bed; in bed, he wants to get out of it. While the incapacitated are understandably dependent on the magic "call button," the individual I am describing is insatiable. He wants something. Anything! Of course, what he really wants is someone to care for him, someone with whom he can *communicate*, someone who says, I know you are alive and I care for you. Someone he can like and turn to.

Other old people read the social signals loud and clear but react very differently. In their vulnerability they retreat from the impinging pain, showing the classic withdrawal symptoms from lack of love. Their relatives visit more and more infrequently, since conversations are forced and trivial. Within the institution they make no friends and speak essentially when spoken to, which isn't often. They may develop a fierce territoriality, guarding or even hiding worthless little mementos. Eventually they do not even watch television or read a daily newspaper or participate in the intermittent "activities" of the institution. The therapist and social director (if there is one) describe them as unreachable. Some are. One old woman who came complete with six relatives, five potted azaleas, and a collection of Dickens was in less than a year spending the days in "her" stuffed chair in the lobby "watching the cars go by." During visiting hours when automobiles cut the streets from view, she became so panicky that the aides would tie her in a wheelchair and roll her down to stare into the empty cement-lined patio. Her family divided visiting chores so that every Wednesday night and Saturday afternoon someone was with her at least a half-hour.

Then there was "the hummer," whose only relative, a married son, lived at some distance. She had been in a convalescent hospital for two years and had not been seen by a physician in the two months I knew her. The staff said she was strong as an ox and they stayed away from her as much as they could. She hadn't a magazine or a book or a photograph in her room. She ate well (the hospital was proud of "good food attractively served"), was kept supplied with more clothes than she needed, and spent her days compulsively rubbing the surface of her bureau, or her tray-table or—anything, and h-u-m-m-i-n-g. Ceaselessly humming. She was eventually moved to a rear room where she could not disturb her neighbors. The night nurse, Miss Caesar, had been there when she was admitted. "She thought she was going for a Sunday ride."

Few individuals, old *or* young, have the resources to withstand prolonged isolation from human contact. "Solitary confinement," whether self-imposed through a sense of powerlessness or unworthiness, or dictated by a rejecting culture, spells defeat in the aging game. On the other hand, creating access to sources of affection, to love and be loved, is a critical tactic of successful aging.

Love, however defined, involves a series of acts. It does not thrive in passivity, but withers and dies. The reciprocal exchange of love is critical to healthy living and to successful aging. We know that babies who are physically well nurtured cannot mature into emotionally normal adults if they are unloved during the first years of life: their physical well-being is dependent upon the continuing circumstance of love. And the af-

116

fectionless character that results from forced adaptation to a loveless existence is now widely recognized as a prelude to mental illness or the compensatory revenge of juvenile delinquency.

The old need love too, not just attention. The institutionalized old come to manifest the same kind of physical and emotional stultification that has been described for loveless children. Further, it is the need to love, as much as the need for love, that is critically linked to the capacity for *basic physical survival*. People cannot live without loving—actively loving someone, something, some ideology that can be translated, in terms of hours of the day, days of the week, months of the year, into a code of action. The effect of lovelessness on the personality is severe. The prolonged absence of love atrophies, sealing off one by one motivations to please, to remain informed, to innovate and plan, motivations that keep the mind active, and muting that sense of worth we need to see confirmed in the judgment of someone we care for. Without someone to care for we forfeit ego strength.

For life to endure into new decades, we must insure that love too endures. Strategically, it means establishing new sources of intimacy to replace those time or society chooses to strip from its aging members. The old themselves must do this, anticipate this need. And the tactics involved in developing, or maintaining, a rewarding level of intimacy in late life are of two kinds: one is concerned with dispelling fears about continued heterosexual contact, particularly about sex and sexuality; a second, with learning the positive strategies involved in loving and being loved after sixty. The following pages are concerned with the understanding and mastery of these tactics.

Dispelling Fears

The old are all too often afraid to talk with one another, afraid of casual contact, afraid to touch one another, afraid or uninformed about how to initiate or sustain the simplest level of caring personal relationships. Loneliness is rooted in this reticence. So are the narrowness of life and frugality of experience that all too often intensify as men and women age. Where previously casual conversations were automatic in daily living, now a curtain of formality may descend, hampering easy exchange. Many feel constrained in gestures of simple courtesy and are troubled in situations designed for sharing. Esther Kane went to church socials but avoided introductions because "I'm not awfully good at conversation anymore." Jerry Morrell refused a dinner invitation from a woman he admired but confessed he really didn't know why. And Meg McLaughlin avoided a favorite bookshop because "I keep running into this very nice man."

We are all selective in launching conversations with strangers. But many of the men and women with whom I spoke were frank in expressing their fear of how to proceed in social situations with people who appealed to them, with whom they would like to have talked. Widows and widowers sometimes felt curiously ill at ease in situations in which, in previous years, they had moved with easy confidence as married persons. Often they simply did not know how to manage an appropriate level of communication.

Mr. Jaeger, sixty-two, terminated his initial interview with our research project staff after a restless ten minutes, because, he subsequently protested, "I'm not good at talking with young women anymore." The interviewer was forty years of age.

When asked what was the hardest thing about his life today Mr. Carpenter unhesitatingly said "loneliness." He would like to find someone who shares his interest in music but feels he is "too old to be with young women and too young to be with the old." It is, he conceded, "pretty hard to find company."

Quint Beery was awed when he drove a neighbor to the airport and she spontaneously kissed him good-bye. "She just brushed her lips against mine and got on the plane, and in a rush of memories I realized how devoid my life had become of warm human contact. It was the most innocent gesture on her part, believe me. So casual and un-self-conscious that she would have been aghast to learn how much I dwelled on it, how long I thought about the little intimacies so routinely a part of other people's lives and so absent from mine."

This attrition of opportunities to be close to others in friendly but inconsequential exchange, to touch and embrace and laugh, to share secrets, to celebrate or console, to feel particularly masculine or feminine—the diminution of these vibrancies of life—leave us with a wooden sense of impotence. The infrequent glimpses of a more intimate life—a life that could be or might have been—all too often engender the fear that love in the future as in the present will be denied us, perhaps should be denied us for reasons we do not fully comprehend.

Sex and the Experts

In facing the frightening challenge of sexual intimacy in late life, the old have had little help from the experts. In the definition and resolution of problems relating to sex and sexuality gerontologists have largely defaulted. Books on aging, even the most authoritative, usually are either devoid of sections on sexual behavior or allow token reference to it. A major four-volume work on aspects of aging throughout the world allows less than a page to the subject in over 2,500 pages of text. With some notable exceptions, the major contributions have come from outside the field of gerontology itself. Even in the innovative work of Kinsey in the 1940s and the controversial studies of Masters and Johnson in the late 1960s, comprehensive exploration stopped with middle-aged persons. The sixty-seven "aging females" observed by Masters and Johnson were by definition over forty. Only eleven were past sixty. For men the "aging" threshold was upped to fifty—an interesting commentary in itself, and half of the thirty-nine aged men observed in sexual intercourse were less than sixty. The authors themselves were aware of the limitations of their laboratory approach to the study of sex. They emphasized the need to match clinical considerations with scrutiny of the psychosocial adjustments that confront the sexually-oriented older man or woman, and in their recent work have pioneered investigations on the normal, beneficial, and pleasurable aspects of sex among men and women of seventy and eighty. Within gerontology, the work of Robert N. Butler and Myrna Lewis is exceptional. They have emphasized the need for warm and mutually satisfying sexual relationships among the old, and provide the first sexual guide for love and sex after sixty, discussing a range of topics from positions in intercourse to the deleterious side effects on sexual potency of many widely used drugs.

All these specialists, however, emphasize that we are only beginning to learn about the nature of sexual interest and the forms that sexual activity takes in late life. That our knowledge remains so limited is astonishing when we consider the emphasis on sex in our current literature and the popular interest in explicit accounts of what to know and what to do for sexual fulfillment in other life periods.

Limited insight into the sexual needs of older men and women has all too often created the disturbing consensus among many professionals that late life is characterized by the disappearance of sexual needs, impotency, or, at best, disinterest in physical intimacy.

Dr. Butler has pointed out that physicians graduated from medical schools before 1961 had no formal training in sex education and that even today many have no understanding whatsoever of the special problems of sex in late life. Dr. Mary S. Calderone, veteran expert on human sexual behavior and champion of liberated approaches to aging and sex, has warned that "through sheer ignorance" physicians themselves can pass on destructive attitudes when they become aware of a "sexual problem" with an older patient. Women after hysterectomies or menopause have been informed that their sexual lives are over. "So have men in their fifties who have experienced one or two episodes of impotence and gone to their physicians in anxiety." What they should be told is that most sexual problems in old age are of psychological rather than purely organic origin and are almost always remediable. Above all, absurd myths of the inevitable linkage of old age and sexual decline should be dispelled.

Not surprisingly, many men and women are today unclear about their continuing identity as men and women, and for the most part are as apprehensive about their future sex life as teenagers. Actually the positions are quite analogous; both are in the dark as to what to expect of the opposite sex and as to what is expected of them.

"It *is* just like adolescence," said Gina Rowles of her reactions to courtship at sixty. "You just don't know what's happening to you." In some cases, sexual attitudes seem almost to be reactivations of preadolescent ones and echo those early discomforts in boy-girl relations. Irma Jacobi, a widow of sixty, observing behavior between elderly men and women in her apartment building said: "There are no men I dislike except those downstairs. Why, they don't treat women right. They've lost their desire for women and have got it against them, I guess. In the lobby all the women go with heads up and won't talk to them." With a younger cast the scene could be out of a television script, conveying the poignantly comic mixture of attraction and rejection that characterizes uncertain teenage encounters.

Hurdles to Sexual Adaptation

The major hurdle to satisfying sexual adaptation in old age lies in the devastating popular (and sometimes "scientific") mythology that has grown up around sex after sixty. The "normal" man or woman over the age of sixty is assumed to be de-sexed. The post-sixty American, hence, is neither attracted to the opposite sex nor does he evoke their interest. He cannot. The sexual drive associated with youth is regarded as having properly tapered with middle age and vanished in happy coincidence with the end of sexual attractiveness at sixty—by the most generous estimate. A few notable exceptions are regarded as sexually "fixed" still in the semi-vigor of middle life. The individual who has not yet figured this out and continues to display more than platonic interests may be regarded as a dirty old man or a nymphomaniac. Such people wind up, or should, in psychiatric wards. The most charitable version of this social stance is a view of older men and women as having entered a neuter zone, like dime-store dolls, virtually devoid of sexual identity except for the "safe" concomitant clues of dress and hair style. Most are regarded as having reached a unisexual level of identification, a condition projected for all of us by Rudy Gernreich, the designer: by the year 2000 we shall, with the first evidence of aging, cover our previously bare *young* bodies with tent-like robes, and men and women, with shaven heads, will go about indistinguishable from one another. Signs of this extreme neutering—unisex—process are already with us.

A social worker, responding to my written question about the progress of a patient after his months of psychiatric confinement, put a penned note in my office mailbox. "Subject," it read, "is clearly happy to be back in familiar surroundings, but is cautious about making future plans. Its health is good, and needs appear to be met."

The desexing of old men and women appears, at first glance, out of keeping with the current direction in sexual mores. In the Western world today we are busily dissolving all social forms that interfere with the free and highly individualistic expression of sexual interest. Rather than regulate sexual activities to preserve an established social system, as is the case in most of the non-Western world (through caste, clan, or family regulation of mating patterns), Americans today may have sex inside, outside, or instead of marriage. The unwed mother, hidden two decades ago, enjoys the limelight. Movie and television celebrities are emulated and adored in their disdain for marriage and "proper" alliances. Social control is increasingly viewed as social bondage in matters sexual as well as civil. In brief, sex wags the system. Whether the consequences to the in-

123

dividual are psychologically rich or threatening is debatable, and speculation floods the literature, but many social consequences are already clear. The liberated American has come to be viewed incontrovertibly as a sexy American. Further, in our competitively oriented world sex and success have become laminated. Falling short of either perfect sex or perfect success suggests a kind of impotence on both counts.

But the old person is as short on sex-potential as he is on success-potential in the judgment of almost every American who is not old. The twenty- or thirty-year-old has prerogatives in the sexual as well as social sphere by the simple fact of youth. Youth is sexy. Age is not.

It may be that as the current innovators of sexual liberation themselves age there will follow greater receptivity to "sexiness" across the life span. As of now, however, any such trend is not manifest beyond one's thirties. With middle age sexuality reaches unnervingly low levels, dipping right off the gauge at sixty. Especially for women.

Men get a little more social yardage. They are physically more durable as sex objects, in part because they are scarcer the older women get. The wrinkle that adds character to a man's appearance, enhancing the image of ruggedness, is devastating to a woman. A wrinkle to her presages the total collapse of face and figure, at least in popular mythology. If you are alert to the refinements of female discrimination, you will find bountiful evidence in the advertisements and prose written for middle-class readers. The short stories of *Good Housekeeping, Family Circle,* and *Cosmopolitan* discriminate chillingly against older women with whom these magazines' readers are obviously reluctant to identify. Thus, in one story our hero's father is, at sixty-three, "disturbingly masculine still, deep crinkles warming the intense gaze of sea-blue eyes." But Martha (judiciously identified as past fifty) "must once have been quite beautiful. Now, colorless and vague physically. I found myself trying to remember the color of her hair and eyes. Those heavily crow-footed eyes."

All in all, the general public believes that continuing masculinity and femininity grow progressively more suspect as men and women age—with sexual credibility greatest in proportion to the individual's proximity to youth. Even among the old, acceptance of sexual interest runs up against baleful suspicions that our lengthened life span has only negative implications for continued intimacy. In the minds of just about everyone—experts included—there must surely come an age when sexual interest is a shameful if not absurd concomitant of life.

This kind of thinking is false. It spells trouble for persons now old and for all of us who *will* be old—for it encourages a social view of the post-sixty population as normatively ,asexual. This posture has dreadful ramifications for the emotional, physical, and mental health of us all.

How We Desex the Old

Spend a little time in a nursing home or hospital and you will get the picture. Birthday parties and lotto games and Yuletide festivities are planned ideally for mixed groups, and it is regarded as cunning to see the old-timers dressed in their best and perhaps a little more socially attentive than usual of one another. Old men in special-occasion sport shirts are joshed about their slicked-down hair. Women are as carefully coiffed, beribboned, and jeweled in their costume earrings and brooches as the overworked attendants can manage. But it is all like the playhouse fun of nursery school; no one expects any real heterosexual involvement, and the simplest kind of overture evokes a giddy staff reaction.

Miss Reynolds, the social director of the Rainbow's End Rest Home, supervised the activities of fifty-eight men and women whom she considered "just darling, every one of them." The biggest event of the month was the third-Saturday "Golden Get-together," when the red geranium was moved from the dining room to the "rumpus room," and two long streamers of lavender crepe paper were removed from the top of the bookcase and strung the length and width of the room. The craft class made name tags: pink for the ladies and blue for the men, with last names written in great printed letters and pinned to the front of shirts and blouses or of robes for those not well enough to dress.

"Actually," said Miss Reynolds, "the wheelchair patients are the least troublesome and sometimes have the most fun. The others sometimes get carried away and can present problems." Dancing is discouraged.

"It is disruptive and you have to *watch* them. Some of the ladies get silly and before you know it you have these little rivalries going and it doesn't make for group harmony."

Joan Carmichael was pointed out as something of a worry. "She's only sixty-three and rather pretty, and unless the evenings are really structured, we have problems. Sometimes we have slides, and last week we played a break-the-balloon game. We try to keep them in the same places each time. Of course, when we have folk dancing, then they are all together and that's a different thing."

126

She clapped her hands to quiet one rather noisy, mingling group of about six: "Boys and girls—ice cream is served."

In the rare circumstance that a liaison of some permanency does develop, it is regarded as having threatening consequences for everyone. In one small institution (not a mental one), I watched with interest the development of a warm friendship between a rangy Irishman of about seventy-five and a plump little woman in her late sixties.

Ed Gallagher was well liked. He had a vigorous, good-humored way about him and he walked the long corridors with a bouncy gait that suggested he was about to go into a full sprint. A great storyteller, he specialized in anecdotes of Irish priests and Jewish mothers and Italian bootleggers—all in dialect and fully dramatized. But he didn't like the home. He was there recovering from a mild heart attack. A widower, he had planned to return to his son's home where he had lived for five years, but the son's wife was exerting all possible influence to keep him in the rest home. And the old man was beginning to get the picture.

The woman, Angie Sturiale, was Italian-born and after forty years in this country still had a fearful accent and confused most of her conversations by misusing pronouns. She had been devastated by the death of her husband and had been brought to the home in a state of deep despondency after two years of going it alone in a large suburban home. Her only daughter had in the meantime managed to sell her mother's home, so that now she found herself without a place to go.

Angie was a made-to-order audience for Ed's stories. He could make her laugh uproariously by poking fun at her "Italianness," and he felt a certain privilege about doing it because his wife had also been Italian. Both were fervent Catholics and had small shrines alongside their beds, complete with little bottles of holy water, a rosary and pictures of the saints, and holy cards with prayers on them.

They would sit in the lobby after breakfast sharing Ed's daily paper, and she talked him into watching three of her favorite programs ("Gunsmoke," Lawrence Welk, and Lucille Ball). His health improved and he was able to eat in the red-carpeted dining room (Spanish-modern, the institution's joy, and on any inspection tour by families of prospective inmates, prima facie evidence of the toniness of the rest home). Eating side by side at one of the tables for eight, they talked endlessly about their families and past lives and buoyed one another with more hope than conviction that their current problems would disappear and life would be free and good again. It was a long time before it was evident to the staff (the patients *knew*) that these two were increasingly together not by chance.

The Italian woman, despite her earlier grief, was naturally effusive, hugging doctors and nurses when they came and left, and this had brought amused smiles and little hand pats in return. But the alarm went off when she and the Irishman were caught *holding hands* in his room as they sat looking out onto the cement patio with its limp little pepper tree.

Nobody knew what to *do*. But clearly something had to be done, as Mrs. Betz, the director of the home said, "before this thing gets out of hand." The next time the Irishman's son and the Italian woman's daughter came in Mrs. Betz brought them (separately) into her office and told them all about what she thought "really amounted to no great problem at this time." But, as she said, "they both have problems enough already." I was asked to be present, as a kind of witness, "just in case there is ever any question about it or the home." Mrs. Rinaldi (Angie's daughter) saw it all as the final evidence of her mother's incompetence and in a matter of days was granted power of attorney over her mother's remaining assets. The Irishman's son brought his father home with him. "For a while anyway. Poor old Dad." As it was, the Irishman succumbed after a second powerful heart attack followed by pneumonia.

In the hospital he asked to see me. It was less than a week before his death. I had to hide my shock at the great weight loss. But his eyes were bright and he had that familiar good humor.

"I was wondering if you would do something for me," he said. "You know, it's hard for Angie to get here and I really didn't expect it."

When I offered to do what I could and bring her if there were a way, he said: "No. It isn't that. But you could give her something. My rosary. It's from Lourdes. She's got one from Fatima. We always figured that when we prayed together it was a sure thing. Well, it's too late for me. . . ." And when I started to protest he waved his hand in a way that made me ashamed I had tried to fool him with the contrived deceits so familiar to all institutionalized old people.

"I would just like her to have mine. My rosary. Now. If I wait, well, it won't go to her regardless of what I say. Will you bring it to her? Say it's for her birthday. I used to rib her. 'Happy Birthday,' I'd say. And when she's say it wasn't her birthday, I'd say, 'I know, I just like to be early.' And don't tell her I look like hell."

Those two people, who could have enriched one another's final days and perhaps each lived a little longer, were crushed by separation, were judged mentally un-balanced because they fell simply and slowly and warmly in love.

Positive Strategies

Think of sexuality as composed of the characteristic attitudes and responses of men and women toward themselves and toward one another as men and women; and of sex as the whole gambit of emotional bodily involvement from hand-holding to copulation, which is both a product and a catalyst of physical attraction between the sexes. A growing literature on body symbolism emphasizes the obvious interdependency of sexuality and sex. The message, "I am interested in you," is relayed—often unconsciously—by precise gestures or postures of face and body. When words are premature or difficult, an attentive smile, the solicitous lighting of a cigarette, or "open" body stance can speak volumes. Sex is a part of love even in old age: the nearness of a loved one, the feel of a loved one, the full involvement of mind, emotions, and body, if and when you want it.

How do men and women who *want* to bring sex into their lives accomplish it in their sixties and beyond, particularly in the face of an unsupportive, often hostile, society? Obviously those among the old who accept the consensus that they are beyond sexual needs—or are demeaned by them—will not be successful in finding love in late life. The Luthers and Lucilles of this world, however, are off to the right start with the unassailable conviction that age, not sex, is the transient dimension of life. And they live with an abounding, and self-fulfilling, confidence in their right to enjoy one another and their own bodies. They view themselves as ren-

130

egades, happily opposing our uncharitable mystique about late-life sex and sexuality wherever they find it.

Luther told me that when he shopped for a nightgown as a birthday present for Lucille, the clerk brought out an armful of flannel gowns. "Hell, lady," he told her, "I'm shopping for my girl friend, not my mother." He bought a black lace gown with satin slippers to match.

The idea that it is appropriate for the old to want love and to seek it out is something that Nan Buckner, a divorced woman of sixty-three, believes should be widely championed. "At least those who care about us could remind us that we are still attractive as men and women, that we should be concerned with looking our best, and that there is indeed much hope for new opportunities to love and be loved. Instead, for months and months after my divorce everyone from my minister to my sons was 'helping me' adjust to life alone— apparently forever."

Her family and friends, she said, "*were* a huge help in the early weeks when I simply needed to be with someone—anyone." But after a year Nan chafed at her loneliness.

"The whole world seemed bent on convincing me I'd reached some kind of impasse that I was just too dullwitted to accept. I grew more, not less, depressed. I felt so desperately frustrated." It seemed to Nan that there had to be an alternative to accepting the end of meaningful male companionship.

"You know it takes determination to hold on to your pride and your integrity as a woman and to resist the pressures to think what the heck, I *am* over the hill. It takes courage to know yourself, to accept your desires for companionship and love and sex as natural and healthy, and to go after what you want."

131

She smiled, enjoying her story. "I stopped brooding and started moving."

She had some money "put away for a rainy day." And she decided that day had come. "I found a reliable beauty salon and indulged myself in a general overhaul—a new hair style and some lessons on how to make the most of my features with the proper makeup and grooming. I gave away a half-dozen dresses I'd been wearing so long I was sick of them. Instead I worked out a budget that would let me buy one absolutely chic outfit each season so that I'd feel really good about myself and my femininity."

She was not shy about expressing to her friends her interest in meeting some eligible and absorbing men. "My daughter thought it all smacked of degeneracy or second childhood, but I told her exactly what I told my relatives and friends: 'I am no more interested today than I was thirty years ago in limiting my social contacts to the female of the species.' "

Having decided that "no man was going to break my door down finding me," Nan made herself "as socially visible as I could." She had always regretted having no proficiency at any sport and decided to take up two that particularly appealed to her and that also seemed tactically promising.

"I found out that—on a guest basis—you could take golf lessons at the country club, and that there was a public skeet-shooting range out near Lake Merced." She proved fair at both sports, and eventually found herself a part of mixed gold foursomes as well as accepting the solicitous assistance of weekend shooting enthusiasts.

Having always regretted that her former husband did not share her desire to travel, she now began making plans to do so. Cruise ships were too expensive so she chose instead the adventure and camaraderie of small-group treks closer to home. "After all, I'm in excellent health and I think small groups are chummier anyway. Fourteen of us rafted down a river in Oregon and at night we talked around the campfire and slept under the stars. Four of us were fifty-five or older and there was a lot of exchanging of addresses." She took a field course at a local college that brought twenty amateurs out in a ship to explore the sea life off the Farallon Islands. "Afterwards, some of us would go out to dinner at fun places down by Fisherman's Wharf."

She learned, she said, "studiously to avoid garden clubs, tea parties, and fashion shows."

Eighteen months later she told me: "I confess I sometimes thought I was getting in over my head. I had never thought of myself particularly as an outdoors woman. But you find out a good deal about yourself when you get into new things. I'm convinced it is the only way to feel alive and remain involved with people. I've loved every minute of it."

She hasn't married. "I'm not sure now that I really do want to marry—though I confess that was probably uppermost in my mind when I started all this. I only knew I didn't want to spend the rest of my life alone or in a world of women.

"I have men friends," she said. "Close, good friends. I surprised myself when I turned down one proposal of marriage." She laughed. "Would you believe I told him that I don't think I'm ready for it!?"

She enjoys her home where she now entertains "very informally, but much more often than I used to. And, if I need an escort for a party or play, there is almost always someone I can call. I discovered to my surprise that there are attractive, interesting single men just as eager for warm, intelligent companionship as I was."

From time to time she has dated men younger than herself. "Some as much as twenty years. Why not? The older you get, the scarcer men your own age, they tell me. I'm vital and healthy. I like the attention of accomplished, interesting younger men, and—though I may not talk like it—I'm very cautious about all the attachments I make. None of these swinging singles places for me. But it's about time the sexual revolution reached those of us most in need of the changes it brings."

Of her sex life she says, "I am not promiscuous. But at my time of life no-strings arrangements with men I like and respect, who care for and respect me too, make sense—perhaps more than they do for the young. After all, maturity and experience are not the worse preparations for a happy sex life."

Sexual Activity in Late Life

In the aging game dispelling personal fears and social stereotypes about sex and aging depends, in part, on more informed views on sexual activity in late life.

Our own research with 1,200 men and women supports a malleable and optimistic view of sex in late life. Although sexual desire (and potency among men) diminishes significantly from seventy to eighty years of age, an active sex life is normative into the seventies. The diminution is gradual. For men surviving into their eighties continued sexual activity was reported as no great rarity, though none reported having sexual intercourse oftener than once a month.

"You have to work a little harder, that's all," said Cy Hart, who had remained sexually active until the death of his third wife when he was eighty-five.

The significantly lowered sexual activity of older women generally follows from the increasing unavailability of partners, as with advancing age women out-live their spouses and men friends, or as men seek younger sexmates. There are five times as many widows as widowers in the United States. Also, the decline of intercourse for the female may also be more a reflection of the potency of her mate than of her own. For, as Masters and Johnson have shown, the post-sixty female is fully capable of orgasmic response in sexual performance, particularly if exposed regularly to effective sexual stimulation. The work of Kinsey and his associates is corroborative.

Men appear more vulnerable than women to physiological influences on the expression of sexual behavior. While these influences are far from understood, they are known to involve the hormone level of the individual, the brain centers controlling sexual response (a specific center for erection of the penis has been identified), and alterations within the central nervous system's control of sexual behavior. However, evidence is impressive that the gradual decline that takes place in the sexual activity of men also reflects the influence of powerful non-physiological factors.

Men are apparently less active than they would like to be and constitutionally can be because of social brakes on sexuality after sixty. Widowers risk the dirty-old-man label, especially in overtures to younger women. Making overtures to any woman is often threatening to an already wavering self-esteem, and diminishing drives do not always provide sufficient impetus to overcome the uncertainties of these psychologically hazardous new undertakings—although some men in our study group reassured themselves of continuing potency through an almost compulsive promiscuity.

Living in poverty makes for very poor dating. Lack of privacy in rooming-in arrangements with sons and daughters means few can pursue anything beyond the most superficial kind of social exchange. The inaccessibility of transportation and the danger of venturing forth with a date on night-time streets; the marginal nutritional intake that often lowers physical vigor and enthusiasm for entering new relationships; the trauma of near-flophouse living that makes it difficult to be anything but a loner—all these circumstances and more inhibit what should be the easy, slow, uncompromising flow of men-women relationships into late life.

And overriding everything is a yet more negative influence: the social suggestion, powerful in its subtlety and pervasiveness, that the old are beyond these needs.

Widows and widowers run into the greatest problems precisely because their interest in continued sexuality becomes more visible than that of married older couples or people who have never married.

No one really knows or thinks about how sexually active cohabiting older mates are. (More than younger people think; that much is statistically demonstrable.) But when men and women elect to seek one another out, to enter at sixty-five or seventy into the conversation, dress, and proximity that send up clear signals of mutual interest, then the alarm sounds for their younger family members and friends.

Marriage at Sixty-Four

Gina Rowles confided that she never told her son and daughter, who live at some distance, of her marriage plans. "I know they would have been dreadfully concerned and probably tried to dissuade me. George and I called them on our wedding day and told them they were invited to celebrate with us when we got back from our honeymoon. I didn't tell them we were going to Hawaii. By the time we got back I'm sure they realized there was nothing they could do about it."

After some initial embarrassment, she spoke with me about her sex life.

"I was raised in the South, you know, and for me love has always been perhaps a more romantic and dreamy thing than it should be, given all the pressures of life today. I loved my first husband very much, but he was a domineering man and with considerable sex drive, I think, but . . . well, rather unresponsive to my needs. Though he didn't mean to be. I never seemed really to be *with* him. Sex was something that just went along with marriage, with being a good wife—and I was a good wife and we did have a good marriage. But I can't say I felt frustrated or anything in terms of sex when I found myself without it."

Her sexual adjustment to a second marriage at sixty-four to a man of seventy-two was a very different story. A bride of two years when I spoke with her about her sex life, she was obviously and radiantly happy.

"I was quite afraid of it actually. Sex. Not that I dreaded it or anything. It was more a lot of little things that I felt so unsure of." She laughed. "Later on, when George and I talked, he told me he was the same way. He's a widower.

"Your body is different. And you look in the mirror and wonder what he will think of it now. You haven't the same appeal, you think. There's so much more sag, more weight too—though I did lose fifteen pounds and that made such a difference.

"We weren't really intimate until three days after our marriage. It was a gradual thing. I think we both were very protective of one another. But it was a very special and happy time. Being close, the feel of warm bodies, falling to sleep with our arms around each other. Little

137

by little. Maybe that's the way it should always be, I don't know."

She wasn't sure how to answer the question about frequency of intercourse. "It varies is what I mean. Sometimes he feels readier than at other times, I guess. It's not like when you are twenty. But we make love when we want to, maybe every ten days or two weeks. We are good together and I don't think either of us has ever been happier."

Love is Therapy

Love is good therapy in the post-sixty years. It is true that ill-health, infirmities, and poverty create special problems for the heterosexual activities of the old. But even in combination, these circumstances do not render the old incapable of loving or being loved. Or of thinking of themselves as still attractive *men and women*. On the contrary, such circumstances make love a more critical need for the continuation of life, meaningful life. The stalemate occurs when these problems, where they exist, are not considered relevant. Age *is* considered relevant. The young don't *think* about whether the old love or are loved. It is often simpler if neither circumstance obtains.

The conspiracy against sex and sexuality for the old is an extension, and a critical one, of the basic social design for the disengagement of America's old. Desexing further assures their dehumanization. It further contributes to their social nothingness.

That there is life and will and investment in the future among the old disturbs most Americans, though they will not admit to it or perhaps even consciously consider it. Dating and planning and the welding of destinies suggest an approach to life that challenges the current image of old men and women as quiescent and shelvable. It is inconvenient, too, for many relatives who see babysitters disappearing and small inheritances jeopardized. The old, like children, are regarded as most supportable when least disruptive.

Active older people are also a social nuisance. They are likely to perpetuate their roles within the work force, to seek separate housing even where it is scarce, to demand medical attention for one another for problems that threaten their activity, and to sustain one another's interest in political and social and cultural issues. And to spend what money they have on one another instead of their children or other family members.

Love and sanity go hand in hand after sixty. Not necessarily physical intimacy, or sustained sexual relationships, but the sense of deep regard, devotion, and kindness felt for someone and reciprocated by that someone as a part of love—Robert Louis Stevenson's "passionate kindness," or Ashley Montagu's "vital essence."

"It came to me, all of a sudden," said one gentleman of seventy, "that there wasn't a living soul who could take my hand and call me by my first name." He was Gramp and Dad and Mr. Townsend. But never "John." He missed the continued identification with life and self that comes from the opportunity to see oneself through the eyes of one other human being for whom you care and who cares for you *even though he or she doesn't have to.*

If men and women are to reach out for opportunities to relate to one another *as* men and women, they must find within themselves the confidence to do it. A confidence in their continuing masculinity and femininity and their right to affirm it. The conviction that their bodies like their minds are theirs, to enjoy as they—and no one else—dictate. Continuing links with children, friends, and siblings *are* important in late life and will be discussed in subsequent chapters. But in the aging game the stunning isolation that threatens all our lives after sixty is most vibrantly combated by attention to, and from, a mate—the subject of the next section.

Tactic Five: Develop the Alliances That Count

Strategy for aging involves resources—physical, financial, and emotional. It also involves alliances. Nobody can go it alone. Not successfully.

A MATE

Divide and conquer. It works with the old who, in society's judgment, are better kept at arm's length where they can be picked off one by one. The old person who is single and alone is a ready candidate for forced disengagement from the active, social world. Isolation, we have seen, not only insures the separateness of the old, but weakens their disturbing tendencies to seek relatedness and lessens opportunities for it.

A spouse is the best insurance against this kind of

target practice. A mate is the surest prescription for continuing activity. In successful aging, a basic rule (subject to few exceptions) is this: after sixty, if you haven't a spouse or steady friend, *get one*.

What are the chances for married status in late life? Pretty good for men. Not so good for women. For the sixty-five-and-over population, there are about 145 women per 100 men, or fourteen million women to ten million men.

There are five times as many widows as widowers, reflecting both the longer life span of women and the cultural precedent that regards wives as properly younger than their husbands. Women of fifty or over who form any interest in men five or ten years younger than themselves find the dirty-old-woman label almost automatically applied to them, says Dr. Calderone. Psychiatrists and others, however, have begun to suggest that, for all age groups, the marriage of women to men younger than themselves would contribute to a better balance in stable male-female relationships after sixty. Today, of married men over sixty-five, more than 40 per cent have under-sixty-five wives. Also those post-sixty marriages which do occur are more often successfully initiated by men than by women.

Marriage and Successful Aging

Marriages that last into late life run the gamut from the blissful to the tortured. Yet all reveal something useful as to the strategic implications of marriage for successful aging.

Mrs. Reineke, a wealthy woman, suffers from multiple sclerosis and is confined to a wheelchair. She has an attentive daughter and many devoted friends who are daily visitors. Unhesitatingly, however, she speaks of feeling closest to her husband because of "his love and devotion.

"I know positively I am uppermost in his mind, as he is in mine. He thinks of me first, last, and always in a way that no one else does or can." It is only his love for her and hers for him that draws her back from the brink of suicide, an act she has seriously considered since the rapid worsening of her condition. "Make no mistake," she said. "He is my life now."

Men and women find within their marriages the buffers which they need to cope with the assaults, large and small, of old age. For many, late life itself has become a catalyst for increased devotion and concern. Wives are often men's intermediaries in the community, planning, saving, keeping viable their remaining social contacts and links to distant children. Some men recognize a new need for a stable person to guide them and take some of the responsibility for their actions, even to disciplining them.

"I had an awful time when I first quit work," said Jack Durrell. "Sat around moping, started smoking an extra pack a day, and got a stubble of beard on my chin that would scratch an alligator. Well, Millie, she put up with it for a while, patting me on the back with a 'there, there.' " But about six weeks of that was apparently enough for Millie.

" 'Well,' she says, one fine afternoon, 'it's a kick in the fanny I think you need. You're not dead yet. Now get up and get out and don't let me see your face in here 'til dinner time.' "

After a couple of days of "just walking," Jack developed a routine. In the morning he tries to get in a little physical activity, out-of-doors unless the weather is very bad. "We're not too far from Golden Gate Park and it's beautiful the year round. You can walk or row a boat or see an art exhibit or learn about astronomy. And I talk to all kinds of people."

But what he likes best and has become avid about is lawn bowling. "We play in teams, three to a side. Millie and I were runners-up in the fall tournament. She taught me. And we made some good friends. We all pack lunches and eat near the rose garden. Beautiful. Beautiful. Once a month we have dinner out, the whole gang."

Afternoons have a more sober commitment. "I walk down to Clement Street, Monday through Friday, and relieve Matt at the Diamond Hardware Store. He's alone there in the afternoon, and if I go down he can take a break and go out and have a cup of coffee. I mind the store, so to speak. We used to work together in the contracting business, so I know the stock pretty well." For this, a volunteered service of which he is proud, Jack receives no pay; but from time to time his old friend sees to it that he receives tickets to a ball game, theater tickets, or "something for the house. Matt knows what Millie likes." Jack is secure enough financially to accept this arrangement as one that accrues from his rather than Matt's largesse.

This leveling of interests, and the merging of time, of thought and of selves, reveals a relatively unexplored feature of late-life marriages: the development of a greater equality between partners. Husband and wife appear more as social equals, dividing much of the household labor, blending masculine and feminine chores into one compact domestic unit.

"We live together closely. More than we ever have, since the first days of marriage. But in a different way now. You rarely see us alone, and I guess this affects the way we live and act."

Similarly, Cy Hart recalled the quality of his third marriage at the age of sixty-four, shortly after he lost his second wife. (His third wife was a long-time friend to both of them.) "She was more of a companion to me than the others were. We were in the apartment together, day after day, and we went everywhere together. A team. She was closer to me than my children were. She stood with me forever."

In a way such men and women point the way for all of us to the kind of sexual equality our feminists seek, or say they are seeking. Not a usurpation by the female of male activities, but a restructuring of territory so that the social arena is relatively free of the kind of markers that tend to label our fields of action. Men do not abandon masculinity, nor wives their femininity, but males do not deprecate involvement with the home or sense a diminution of assertiveness. It is a reaching out for new sensitivity, not a decline from grace. Women are less covetous, less defensive and cautious of prerogatives. Actions are not weighed and prejudged to defend a balance of power. There is a muting of the edges of learned, sex-linked temperaments. Men and women are kinder to one another. It is this development which, in large measure, makes late-life marriage an attractive undertaking even for those who have known earlier, less-rewarding unions.

It has something to do with a shifting of priorities, a new defense system. A new crisis, aging, supplants the old, weary little vanities that pit spouse against spouse. Now it's us against them, a declaration of unity as well as war. And with the new crisis there is often a new zest, a heightened awareness of the joy of an unequivocal ally on the personal and social front.

A good marriage contributes to successful aging. A good spouse, one you still like to be with—at least most of the time—is a companion without parallel in the business of living, a reinforcement of the man-woman nature of being that allows each to find satisfaction in the dividends of masculinity and femininity. In a world curiously short of links, one finds an outlet for the continuing need to be needed. At the same time, someone is there to restore flagging spirits, to help in rough times, if they come, and in the small, daily aggravations of life.

A spouse means someone to talk with, to do with, to be with. Strong or weak, quiet or loquacious, a bore or a spellbinder, someone is there at the end of the day. Someone to turn your thoughts out from yourself.

Troubled Marriages

Not all marriages are unmarred by rancor and bitterness, of course. Marriages that in late life fail to build upon or develop potentials of strength and mutual fulfillment are generally unhappy ones and often have long been so. In some, the frustrations and recriminations of years exude like venom to paralyze or destroy.

Rena Baronian is a very bitter sixty-year-old housewife. Her early attitude of dutiful subservience to her foreign-born husband gradually turned into martyrdom, a role played with more blatant histrionics in middle age and finally with fearful depression and cruelty in old age. He is now her nemesis. He stands between her and a final chance at happiness. Happiness to be realized somehow, somewhere—this she will figure out later. But in her perception, it is he, hateful and inescapable, who is the cause of all her unhappiness, of a life barren of fulfillment.

"My husband and I are entirely different people. He's old-fashioned, and I'm modern, creative, different. The trouble is this marriage. It has lasted so darn long. Same old ways go on and on, never ending. When he goes away for a few weeks I begin to feel better."

Despite the intensity of her verbalized hate, the case materials reveal a tortured ambivalence. "For ten years I have hoped for his death . . . but if he *should* die I don't know whether or not I could carry on—alone."

Gene Nathan broods about his long dependency upon a woman he never really loved. His marriage was incompatible almost from the beginning, but their relationship seemed to have stabilized into a kind of mutual tolerance until his wife's forced retirement from teaching. At that point, with Mr. Nathan's own sales career soon to end and with an imminent future of long, shared days together, their relationship worsened.

"For the last five years, it's been hell!" he says. "It's wrong to let a relationship get that way. I let her determine where we lived, where we took trips, our friends. People I liked enormously she just cut off the list. I haven't had a man friend since I got married."

Still, when Mrs. Nathan, engulfed by frustration and mounting depression, was hospitalized, he didn't know what to do with himself. "What do I do presently? Well, I eat supper. Then I go for a walk, and I go to bed at eight at night and get up at four in the morning, simply because I can't sleep any longer. And that's my fascinating life."

A mate is a reservoir of strength and a mirror of weakness. The love/hate, need/rejection theme is present in an impressive number of cases. It is not limited to the disturbed or the institutionalized, and for the most part is not as corrosive as suggested by the example just given. A certain amount of ambivalence is age-linked, a signal of crisis, and normal. Old age brings with it a new perspective not only of marriage, but of the self *through* marriage. In late life, in the often narrowing mirror of social reflection, one's mate becomes an awesome instrument of self-evaluation. Spouses need to be sensitive to their strategic role in their partner's aging adaptation. To many men and women, whether one is more of a person, less of a person, a different person, or a lost cause—a mate's assessment may indeed tell the real story.

"I think I have changed," Jack Durrell commented. "Millie says I've mellowed a bit, not as driven as I used to be and after all—like she says—that's not so bad."

Or, as Mr. Nathan concluded: "If you listen to my wife, the devil wouldn't take me now. I feel so out of things, useless, cantankerous. She remembers the way things were and doesn't let me forget it. I was a pretty good provider in those days."

As aging progresses episodic introspection is common. The *married* me wonders about its identity, fantasizing about the essential me, the separate, the inviolable and alone me. Who am I, apart from, or thanks to, or in spite of this marriage? The right partner serves up positive support and helps a mate in the critical challenge of thinking well of himself or herself *though old*.

In the main, this almost spiritual exercise is related to the extent to which marriage has been a personal refuge as well as a social contract. Good marriages appear to be those that provide a chance for fulfillment at both levels. In the worst marriages, there is a pawning off onto the mate of responsibility, a diversion of blame when self-fulfillment is wanting. But in the nakedness of aging, delay and deviousness of this type won't work. There is no longer that lulling illusion of immortality, nor any justification for the continued postponement of living one's life. For some it is like running through thick wa-

147

ter. They want to *be* now. It is maddening to be frustrated still in long-cherished (if unreasonable) dreams. And the leaden fear is there through the long days and nights that nothing at all lies ahead. And that life is over.

To reach sixty without the conviction of personal integrity, of worth and stature, means we must seek it out then, posthaste, at sixty. And the challenges of aging become unduly confounded by identity crises, a circumstance that can force a stressful dependency upon whatever ties remain, notably spouses, and can permanently inhibit successful aging. It is an unfortunate time to discover that one ultimately is and must be one's own mentor in finding strength or accepting love.

Spouses sometimes feel that they have too much time with one another. Where poverty or sickness further impedes the individual's ability to move freely and widely, the enforced togetherness can, for some, border on the claustrophobic. Where men and women find wide enough involvement, marriages cease to be unnaturally burdened with the whole task of aging adaptation. As Jack Durrell put it: "You can't be happy to come home if you never leave the damn place!" Chronically unhappy, sick marriages should be dissolved well in advance of the demanding togetherness of later life. They seriously impede both partners' chances for successful aging.

Loss of a Mate

Yet even where a marriage has been a stormy one, the loss of a spouse's presence in the home can nevertheless be traumatic. Women must then face the hardest fact of their new position, loss of companionship, whatever the quality, and at a time when they are still quite well

148

and active. During the day, home and friends and mundane small chores can afford some measure of absorption, but in the evening hours they struggle with letdown.

"When the dinner hour comes, I feel sorry for myself, and I'm not the only one. So sometimes I take the bus downtown and have coffee and dessert. It's not being needed. That's the bugbear of all us widows," said Julia Arensberg.

"You need a male companion," Maude Simpson said, "to go to places where you can have fun." And most women still appreciate getting dressed up and being seen in public. Femininity is not discarded with old age, but it is frequently frustrated by it.

Although the loss of spouse brings grave emotional adjustment for some men, they have better opportunities than women to make new alliances: there is a wider market of unattached women, and many men are more disposed to take on a "girl friend" than a wife. Generally these unmarried attachments are of rather permanent nature, with the woman close to the man in age but a bit younger. Examples range, however, from the liaison of a man of seventy with a woman thirty years his junior to that of Angelo Alioto, who in his sixties developed the close companionship with eighty-one-year-old Maude. The sexual scope of these unions ranges from the platonic to cohabitation. Though sex rarely precipitates them, it often becomes an important and continuing part of these attachments.

The process of substitution which we described under Tactic Three (page 52) should be applied in the context of loss of a mate. A woman who is used to having a man around *needs* a man around for all of the reasons she needed him in the first place—and more.

149

She needs an ally in this struggle for successful aging. She needs a friend, a close man friend. This same tactical advantage, these same needs, hold for widowers. But for women, especially those unused to taking the initiative in dating, a good man is hard to find. Our culture offers no incentives or guidelines for the older woman to find companionship and love in late life, and—as we have seen—in its efforts to de-sex the old, male or female, often purposefully impedes the search.

Muriel Garner, shy, feminine, and desolate without male companionship, was eventually goaded into finding a gentlemen friend. At our final interview, a near-psychotic depression behind her, Muriel was a happy woman.

"I can't talk too long. We're going out at five and I have to bathe and dress. I like to take my time so I'll look pretty." Her happiness was real and infectious. She was eager to speak of the changes in her life.

"It was Margie, my hairdresser. You know she kept after me and after me to get out and do things. She wouldn't give me a moment's rest until I cut my hair, and then another thing—all the time—was that I should meet her uncle. Would you believe she set it up? We all went out and then afterwards I did see him a couple of times. Nothing terribly fancy."

She paused and looked at me, almost conspiratorially. "I'll bet you think I married *him*. Well, I didn't. But it got me moving. Got me out." She was enjoying the suspense.

"I invited him to a church potluck dinner. Hadn't been to one in ages but I got this notice and just picked up the phone and said I would come and bring a cake. It was a way of repaying without spending a lot. And *that's* where I met Philip."

She corrected herself. "Well, re-met. You see, he was a

tenant of the apartment house my first husband and I managed. His wife died . . . oh, ten years ago. The four of us knew one another pretty well at one time. But he'd moved away after her death and we'd lost touch."

She talked longer than she had planned, cherishing details of the year-long courtship and marriage and their life together.

"Now I know. It isn't just being married; it's not being alone. And it's a very special kind of love for the both of us. Having someone again, someone to depend on, to help with decisions, to do things with and for."

And then she laughed. "My sister says we're crazy: 'You don't know what you'll get into.' Well, I know what I got out of. And I have known Philip long enough to be sure we are right for one another."

And at the door, as we said good-bye, she put her hand on my arm. "It's a new lease on life, tell them that. Perhaps not for everyone. But it has literally been that for me."

Finding a Mate After Sixty

Where is the best place to look for a mate or a good companion when you are sixty or more? *Not* through agencies. They are fraught with economic and personal perils. A few are good, but most are worthless and some are downright dangerous. Newspaper ads should work but frequently serve up more problems than they resolve. *Not* through old-age clubs where, as a rule of thumb, socializing should be limited to on-the-premise activities or club-sponsored excursions that involve a number of people. Pairing off is fine in this context, but most eligible men and women shy away from "being shopped for" (as ex-marine Vincent Stewart put it) in so blatant a context.

151

One woman had this to say about clubs: "Usually it is not the nice ones who make the moves. There are always one or two Lotharios. Absolute bores. Self-centered. Nobody would have looked twice at them when they were thirty. A new woman comes and you can predict what will happen. Of course, you can't tell her. But after she's served them a meal or two and shared her TV and put up with their repetitious small talk, and furnished the beer, she begins to get the picture. They never come with anything more than a warm handshake and never so much as take you out for an ice-cream cone."

A woman designer I interviewed had an unexpected dividend. She made a friend of a *woman* at an afternoon bridge club. Nine months later she married the woman's brother, a widowed engineer, whom she had met at her new friend's home.

Tactically, a man or woman over sixty is better off in groups that do not signal the age-shared dimension of need. Involvement in clubs based on shared interests or avocations, not on age, does not send up frightening signals. Many over-sixties are shy about calculated "dating," and often are not aware how much they would enjoy man-woman relationships again until they find themselves in them—quite by chance, as it were.

However, in the case of a specific target, a particular person one wants to meet, the direct approach is better than none. George Matthews conspired with his pastor to meet an attractive widow who lived in the same parish. A retired schoolteacher donned hip boots and learned trout fishing to lure a professor whose summer cabin adjoined hers on the Mokelumne River. A librarian arranged for her married daughter to invite a local lecturer—and her—to dinner after a "literary hour." A gentleman of sixty-six, long impressed with the vitality and good humor of his grandson's widowed music teacher, enrolled for piano lessons himself and in eight months married her.

Not all contrived meetings wind up in permanent unions, or should, but they are a start. They get people together, active, planning, taking care of themselves and their appearance. It is good sense, too, to know something of the character and personal history of one's "target." But that information is almost always accessible from someone.

The Unmarried Old

What about the unmarried, those who reach late life without spouses? Should they get one? Are they good prospects? In general, those who have never married or who have delayed a first marriage until the later years of life manifest in their early histories either a strong sense of personal identity based exclusively on work or family, or evidence of long-standing psychosexual difficulties which would make a mature, intimate relationship with the opposite sex problematic at best, and generally ill-advised in old age. They are poor marriage risks.

On the other hand, there is a fascinating minority of men and women for whom the post-sixty years are right for marriage where marriage was not right for them before. Russell Lardner, an apparently confirmed bachelor, put it this way:

"I always knew I'd never make much of a father. Call it selfish or sick. But I knew myself. Oh, I was close a couple of times. But when I was young I was all drive and ambition. I couldn't let go. I simply didn't *want* to marry."

A successful attorney, he has had what he described as "a good and interesting life. I've had good friends, sex pretty much when I wanted it, and the vicarious pleasure of some first-rate nephews and nieces."

Two years ago at fifty-eight he married a widow he'd met at a friend's home. "She's five years younger than I and has a married daughter."

Mr. Lardner finds late-life marriage an almost ideal development.

"I don't see that I'm more 'set in my ways' than anyone. And we are both mature enough to have made what adjustments we needed to. She's beautiful and vital and attentive. And I delight in pleasing her. We have years together. Maybe more than young couples who find their love pulled apart by the exhausting demands of life at twenty, with careers and sex and children and homes to buy and never enough time or money. I've seen it in my work, in a thousand divorce cases. No. The first time around may be best when it's the last and late time around."

It could easily signal a new trend. Late-life marriage with the prospect still of ten to twenty years of life together makes sense. At sixty the social equation is different. The challenge is no less great, and many are readier than they have ever been to devote the bulk of their energies to someone else's happiness.

The socially isolated, the bachelors or spinsters who have maintained a highly restricted social world throughout their lives, function best alone in old age. They have had a lifetime of practice in the self-reliance newly required of so many old people. And having opted for isolation years ago, they scarcely feel ostracized now in later life by the conditions which demoralize those who have been attuned, throughout their adult lives, to more social involvement. Rarely or never close to others, they are spared the grief and loneliness of those who must lose a cherished spouse or child.

But life alone is a precarious and vulnerable business even for them. What is eccentric at thirty may be looked upon as peculiar and dangerous at seventy. Our institutions house thousands who are guilty of nothing more than living too long alone.

Ian Farris spent six months in a state psychiatric hospital and was regarded as one of its more bizarre inmates. His confinement was a source of wonder to him; he felt both sympathy and disdain for the psychiatrists.

"My greatest sin was my visibility," he said later, when he had left the hospital and returned to his flat in a seedy neighborhood off McAllister Street in San Francisco, a section of decaying old mansions. "And I shall not make that mistake twice."

Ian owned the building which he had purchased thirty years before and in which he had lived with his father until the old gentleman died at the age of ninety-two. He had a brief and miserable marriage with "a very difficult lady" when he was fifty and regards himself as a "bachelor actually of long standing."

"I have always had a wide and unusual range of activities which my small income has allowed me to indulge. And I am also a barber. Basically I guess I think of myself as an animal trainer, though I made a mistake obviously in listing my occupation as such."

Over the years he had worked to develop a little act that he staged at children's parties and social clubs and on several occasions in downtown department stores.

"I worked out a routine with cats, birds, and several mice playing together and doing a little acrobatic act. It took me a very long time to perfect it and the children loved it. Twice I gave it at old peoples' homes. Now, of course, it's all fallen apart. I was given no time to see to

155

my animals' care before I was carted off. They simply had them all disposed of."

He was also an inventor of sorts and had spent years working on new uses of plastic, especially for construction purposes, and had several patents. A lifelong enthusiasm was that of growing rare flowering cactus. His small backyard was filled with them, as well as the stairs and every available surface of his house.

"Sometimes I get carried away and work for hours on one thing or another and then I grow neglectful of my appearance and the house. Of course, eventually I just go through it all and clean up."

He was more stunned than bitter about his confinement.

"People are suspicious of a man alone, and the neighbors went into a panic when I invited some of the little children in to see my pets. They phoned the authorities."

He is alone again after his months of institutionalization. More alone than ever. "I can't say that I'm unhappy, not that I particularly want quite as much isolation as I get now. But I suspect I have waited rather too long to try to change things even if I knew how. At forty you're a Pied Piper, at seventy a sick old man."

To sum up, the years after sixty are not the time to be alone, especially if a man or woman has had little practice in it. Isolation, too, easily finishes the dehumanizing action society has already begun. Life slides from a challenge to a holding action to a lost cause.

Satisfaction can be sustained best through a vital, continuing engagement with life in the company of a major ally, a mate—a well-chosen husband, wife, or close friend with whom a mutually rewarding level of intimacy can be evolved and nurtured.

156

Those who cannot or will not choose this route must compensate by preserving a high level of involvement in those contacts that remain or by forging other strong links with the social scene.

Children and grandchildren are thought by some to be the answer. But survival with and through these relatives is tactically complex.

CHILDREN AND GRANDCHILDREN

Julia Arensberg tried to compensate for the loss of her husband by intensifying her relation with her married son. The move to his home in the suburbs cost her the company of friends and the stimulation of a city she loved. And the isolation and tension of daily life with a daughter-in-law who rejected her smothering attentions brought her to the brink of mental breakdown and the final decision to make her way back into a world of her own.

"It was like a pitched camp. But looking back now, I know I was as much to blame as she. Surely more so. I dragged my scars around like a public sacrifice."

It was difficult to imagine in that scene the chic, affable woman who sat across from me, smoking and smiling at what was for her now a tragi-comic image of herself.

"Somehow I thought I could resurrect the past and its joys through my son. God, forgive me. I tried and tried and tried. My happiness, such as it was, was in cooking the things he used to like, talking about the things *we* used to do, dragging out pictures, weeping over records and even TV shows that reminded me of home, Karl, something—anything that's gone!"

She paused and frowned and for a minute, all of it must have been vivid for her again.

"I drove Margaret [her son's wife] up the walls. She hadn't wanted me in the first place and she had made that eminently clear. In a way it made it easier for me to turn from her to my son and my grandchildren."

And then she laughed. "I think I moved out before I was kicked out. Even so, I wasn't brave enough to close all doors too quickly. A visit to my sister in New York, what could be more defensible. And when I came back it was with the courage—not a lot, but enough—to pack *all* my things and go it alone in a small apartment."

She shook her head. "In those first weeks I was sometimes close to panic, but little by little the good moments were more frequent than the bad. In three months I knew I had made it. My only regret was that I hadn't done it sooner."

It is easy to envisage an aging strategy that would build upon a highly accessible and close resource, one's own children, especially when spouse and friends are gone. The majority of older Americans have children. Ninety per cent of all children survive into their parents' sixties. Further, one in three men and women now sixty-five will live out his/her remaining years with three to five surviving children.

Establishing Good Relations

It is, however, tactically unwise to turn to children in late life with the expectation that one can rebuild a world around them, compensating for losses and finding satisfaction vicariously through them. This kind of substitution will not work. The result of such efforts, rather, is more often the dissipation of resources. It creates martyrs, moaners, and hangers-on: Rena Baronian, who felt unloved and whose mouth grew tight and small when she told us there were weeks when her married daughter, who lived an hour's drive away, didn't stop by at all. The retired schoolteacher who ignored his doctor's insistence that he exercise, and would not go to the neighborhood grocery unless his son drove him. And Julia Arensberg, who came so close to abdicating the precious prerogatives of *life* itself. No. Good rapport between the old and their grown children depends basically on the ability of each to manage well *without* the other, especially when they have at least the minimal resources to do so. In our culture there simply cannot be any happy role regressing or role reversals— neither an increasing dependency of a healthy parent upon a child nor the renewed reliance of an adult child upon his post-sixty parent. Our mores do not sanction it; children and parents alike resent it.

Life is best for both generations when they are functioning well and autonomously, even at lower standards of living than might otherwise be possible. Dependence upon one's children in the resolution of aging problems *that can yield to independent action* only alienates the children. Tactical aloofness, on the other hand, frequently invites their attention and concern.

At sixty we cannot expect to depend upon our children for psychic nurturing and basic social activity; we must manage to fulfill these needs by ourselves in other situations. So long as we can and do this successfully we can almost invariably regard our adult children and their families as social allies, as second-string resources of strength in the aging game. Children are additives, sometimes valuable catalysts, in the struggle for successful aging. They will never get you there by themselves.

The greatest damage done in parent-child relations is when one limits the freedom of the other or arouses feelings of guilt. Ideally the child maintains his/her independent dwelling, sustains his/her own family, and achieves according to his/her own standards. The parent is either still with a spouse or has developed an alternative arrangement that makes possible a way of life whose security is not dependent on the dissipation of the child's financial, psychic, or social resources.

Jonathan Holt, a retired successful businessman widowed since the age of forty-eight, has raised two sons and a daughter. He lives alone in the family home. Active and alert and occupied in many activities, he is at seventy-one on excellent terms with his offspring. His children come by regularly and he often drops in on them for visits. In the telegraphic style characteristic of Jonathan's approach, he describes his life with them.

"Same interest in them. But not sitting on top of them. They're mature. I don't interfere. Now they are attentive and don't do it from duty. Good relationship. Different base. See them almost daily."

There is approval of his sons. "Older one does the things I'm interested in. Younger one, I'd have said eight to ten years ago, was a big mistake. Now he's a howling success. They're well on their way."

The values of his own generation, he is aware, might not be suitable for the future his children will face. "There are things I could wish different, but they might not be right for their times. Why should I elect what they do? They are independent as a hog on ice." Of course, Mr. Holt's considerable solvency contributes to his successful adaptation.

At sixty, successful parent-child interaction involves, not a mutual withdrawal from intimate social contact, but an abdication of the potential contest of power and control inherent in the relationship. It works both ways. But the old are most susceptible to taking refuge in imagined prerogatives.

Many of those who become mentally ill have broken themselves in frantic efforts to retain the discipline and influence formerly exerted over their children. When Emilia Carridine's son, Garth, sided with his wife in an argument about his mother's continuous interference in the kitchen, Mrs. Carridine had erupted with a foolish ultimatum. Either her daughter-in-law apologize for what she called her "cruel attacks and senseless jealousy of a mother's place in her son's life," or she would leave that very night.

Four months later when Garth came to the clinic, he talked about it. "It was bound to come," he said. "It was dreadful. I think the worst thing of it was that she had boxed herself in and she knew it. She had come on too strong, but she wouldn't let go. She wouldn't yield an inch."

Garth's wife got the two children into the playroom while he tried to soothe his mother.

"We had had three years of it. Once in a while Georgia lost patience but she took more than she should have. She couldn't do anything right in my mother's eyes; and there was always a steady bombardment of her withering brand of smiling criticism. She knew how I liked my eggs, my shirts, even the temperature of my baths. And she would walk into our bedroom, opening the closed door at any hour of the day or night as though it were the most natural thing in the world. If we went out without her, she would sulk for days; and if we invited her, she had to be coaxed into accepting. Anything that Georgia bought was wrong, and when we went off on vacation without her she had her first in a series of mild 'seizures,' she called them, and we had to drive back from the lake after two days."

Garth tried one last time, that night, to make her understand. "I knew it was hard for her. When my dad was alive it was different. Mother was gracious and easy-going and the house was always full of people. Why, I met Georgia through her. She was her dentist's receptionist. My Mother was crazy about Georgia."

Garth told how he sat his mother down and took her hands and told her they were going to forget everything and have a nice dinner, and maybe relax with a good television show. "We told her we loved her, all of us; but that we had our lives to lead, our decisions to make, good or bad, just as she had hers. But she wasn't even listening. She was like a trapped animal. 'If that's all I mean to you,' she kept saying. And once she said, 'I'll have my way in this, I tell you. I'm your Mother. I'm your Mother!' She scared me." But gradually she quieted and he got her to her room.

"We had to feed the kids, but every couple of minutes I'd tiptoe in. She was lying on the bed, fully clothed. Finally I could tell by her breathing she'd fallen asleep. I covered her and after a while Georgia and I and the kids went to bed."

In the morning his mother was curiously quiet. She sat at the breakfast table but didn't eat. The children were attentive and concerned and she smiled rather flatly at them; then after they went off to school she got dressed and went out.

"She said good-bye almost as though nothing had happened; and after she left I ran in and looked at her things. They were all there. She came home at five o'clock and we had dinner, and then she excused herself

162

and went to her room. I went in once and she was reading. At least she had an open book in her hand."

That went on for three days. What bothered Garth most was that it didn't seem contrived. His mother made no more bids for vindication or apology; she simply smiled when Georgia had told her how sorry she was that she had been so upset. The big confrontation had been on Tuesday and on Friday afternoon he called his mother's physician. He made an appointment to bring her in on Monday. On Saturday night Mrs. Carridine came in to where they were playing cards, put her hand to forehead, and said, "I have been thinking and thinking but there is no place for me to go." And she collapsed.

It was four months before she was released from a mental hospital in her son's care.

The well-adapted old seem able to accept the inevitable loss of power over the young. The loving respect and attention of their children are the most preferred compensations, especially when offered as gifts, dependent only upon the social skills of the old and the gallantry and affection of their children. At its most valued level, parent-child interaction reflects interest and stimulation in one another's company as people first, and as kin only secondarily.

Some men and women develop an almost intuitive feel for the kind of relationship needed: the combination of mutual discretion and empathy, the scrupulous respect, the warm but unprobing interest in one another's activities and goals, a sense of humor, and never, never the melancholy suggestion that love is a debt, one which can at best be inadequately repaid.

The older person sets the tone of the relationship. Often neither child nor parent knows exactly what to substitute now as behavioral guidelines for the twenty or more years of association which our elongated life span affords. The promise of a friend, a dedicated ally, an empathetic chronicler of the changing scene, these are surer incentives than the forced accommodation to an inescapable relative, however special.

Separate Challenges for Men and Women

Men and women face rather different challenges in their associations with grown children. Men are generally less sensitive than women to perceived slights. They are less likely to develop emotional dependency upon their children. Women tend to hypersensitivity about alienation, undoubtedly because so much more of their lives has centered about the home and children. Sometimes the return on their investment seems, in their interpretation, disproportionately meager. Widows often make the mistake of seeking substitution for their husband in a son, who, as Emilia Carridine said, "is all I have left."

On the other hand, men sometimes disastrously insist on advising their children and are more direct in their authoritarianism. In economic and political issues, especially, they tend to regard their views as logical and self-evident, or often take the opposing stands of their children as personal affronts.

"My father thought he could still tell us how to vote," said Gene Nathan's son. "Good Lord, I'm thirty-two and I'm the youngest. He would come over and take out the sample ballot and begin to sing out the yeas and nays on propositions and candidates. The whole thing. When he found out that Harry wasn't a registered Republican he went right through the roof. Harry told him to go to hell, and it really shook the old guy up."

Commanding power over others from the vantage point of a patriarch simply does not work in modern American society, least of all with those who in earlier years have known subservience to him, and have long since grown out of that role.

Women are more inclined to seek and accept the counsel of their offspring, sometimes transferring the authority and judgment of the husband to their own children. They may want the opportunity to nurture and console their married sons whom they may encourage, to the chagrin of daughters-in-law, to turn to them for unrelieved ego recharging in the face of the everyday give and take of busy marriages. "Mother still understands." It does not make for mutual popularity in the son's home, as Emilia Carridine painfully learned.

If there is a law of psychosocial dynamics operating here, it is that late-life satisfaction in parent-child relations will be in direct proportion to the extent to which both abandon the parent-child frame of reference in interaction with one another and substitute a different basis for mutual involvement.

The Strategy of Dependency—If It Comes

Within the minds of many fathers and mothers is the thought that perhaps a day *will* come when one might have to move in with one's children. A few have gone to considerable preparation to avoid it. One woman of Swedish birth has, at some sacrifice, banked her late husband's insurance so as to insure the rather costly membership and maintenance fees of a small Scandinavian residence club, where she will be comfortable and involved whenever independent living grows too taxing. An ex-Navy nurse will use her eligibility for a nurse's retirement home rather than accept the invitation of a married daughter (with whose family she has a warm, close relationship). Both women anticipate a perhaps different but happy style of life in a congenial community of peers.

It is the men who show the greatest reluctance to move in with married children. They consider it evidence of personal weakness. In their maleness they respond with special vigor to threats to culturally prized autonomy, cling to independence for as long as they can make it last. Some hide undernourishment, pain, and failing hygiene in order to avoid it. Even the indomitable Cy Hart, at ninety-three, with his multiple ailments, expressed his pride in independence. This man lives alone. He is on excellent terms with his married daughter and her husband and visits them in Seattle twice a year; but he will not live with them.

"They are both very lovable persons and I know they care for me. They want me to come, but I won't go until I positively have to. Even at my age my security lies here in the neighborhood and house and with the friends I'm used to." Cy has drawn courage from living according to his belief that "when children marry they form a separate unit. Their attachment to their parents is given up. And vice versa. It was the same for me. They are there. I know that. But I'll wait for the nine-count."

This stance is very American. And it is feasible tactically so long as the vindication of separateness is not paid for in misery. Cy Hart will be ready for help when he needs it. He wishes it were otherwise, but he will face adaptation with his familiar dignity, with optimism and confidence. He will be at peace with himself. "I will know that it is time to accept more fully their love. I will make the best of it, for us both."

It is one thing realistically to consider the future. It is

quite another to sicken oneself with tortured reveries of problems that may never arise. Sick daydreams about future dependency are dangerous indulgences. They drain energies and warp personalities in their open invitations to paranoid fantasies and hypochondriacal obsessions. Often serious social repercussions follow. People who become phobic about the future rarely have time for the present. Or pleasure in it. In their dread of eventual dependency (a condition they envisage darkly as synonymous with rejection and despair) and in absurd efforts to avoid it, they often expend the very resources that keep them self-sufficient. Many alienate their children in twisted vindication of the abuse they anticipate at their hands. With dreadful sureness they invite the disaster they shape for themselves.

Actually the errors in their logic have a social, rather than personal, source. We are agreed as a nation that independence is a good and glorious thing. But why do we reason so automatically that dependence is dreadful and reviling? Foreign observers of the American scene, from Alexis de Tocqueville to the Beatles, have wondered at our propensity for black-and-white equations. Success is marvelous, failure is dreadful. Wealth is good, poverty is evil. The new is desirable, the old a repugnant burden. And with awesome ease we extend the adjectives from the deed to the doer, never dismayed by the implications of our stringent illogic.

Independence is a consensual fantasy anyway. None of us is or ever has been wholly free, not psychically, not politically, certainly not socially. It is a question of balance, of will, of the vagaries of life, genetic inheritance and *age*. We treasure our ability to cope with these influences and label our relative success as independence. We should treasure, too, our ability to anticipate some inevitable measure of compromise and to welcome support from our fellows when the struggle goes against us—for whatever reason. Independence and dependence are *not* mutually exclusive conditions.

It is in their interest and in that of their children that older Americans look to and protect their continuing hold on autonomy, but mutual interest is also served when both regard themselves as allies if the going gets too rough. "You can drown at thirty as well as at sixty," said one gentleman. "All the quicker if you don't know when to yell 'help.' "

Relations with Grandchildren

Perhaps the best approach to grandparental strategy follows the line of least resistance. There are periods of life and areas of interest in which communication and mutual reward are considerable between grandparents and their grandchildren. And, there are times and circumstances for both when being together is a bore. Successful adaptation requires learning how to identify these times. Important too is a tolerance for the bleaker, less successful encounters with grandchildren (and their parents). Sometimes it takes practice.

Grandmothers seem to have special slots in the affection of many children, and the happiest are those who have figured out where their strengths lie.

"It's a mistake to try to *use* them," said a grandmother of four, "to make them provide meaning to your life or to hope to become central in theirs. I'm a kind of escape hatch. I can console and pamper and indulge them, but I haven't the real responsibility for their development. And once in a while, when I am serious, they listen."

She has learned not to overreact to lapses from grace. "They want to learn on their own. That's natural. You're a sage to them at four, but you can't really expect to be at twelve."

When she moved out of her son's home, Julia Arensberg found curiously that her relations with her grandchildren improved. "You wear thin if you're always underfoot. And, you know, they sense the tension when two grown women *know* in their secret hearts what is best for them. Sometimes I was downright jealous. It made for hellish living. And kids are quick. They play us all off one against the other. Now I am with them when I want to be; and they are a lot more manageable. I'm sure their mother finds it that way too." And she added, somewhat sheepishly, "I don't have to feel like I'm avoiding work when I just put my feet up and watch them play."

Despite their great love for their grandchildren, the best adapted grandmothers do not allow themselves to become absorbed in the drudgery and minutiae, the constant pressure and vigilance which the very young demand. They've *done* that. "I had my turn. I'm damned if I'll take my daughter's," said Maude. They neither want it nor find it appropriate to their own life stage. And they will not buy time with their grandchildren on this basis.

Many feminine interests have a special invulnerability to change that these grandmothers may capitalize on. Cooking, sewing, good housekeeping, mastering etiquette and feminine grace, an appreciation of art and music—these are timeless absorptions. For most women, pleasure lies in the doing and teaching of these to their granddaughters. Some women who shrink from imposing themselves on their own children feel an affinity with grandchildren. Grandchildren cross over the remembered trials and slights and raw areas that can mar parent-child relationships. And they allow a kind of vicarious rebirth.

"I can see my granddaughter going through some of the same things I did," said a woman of sixty. "She is interested in painting and many of the same things I am. It is a delight to see her discover and take joy in her own femininity. I help her experiment. And it keeps me on top of things."

Rena Baronian, who feels ill-treated by just about every living relative, confides: "I like my granddaughter coming here to me the best. I think she is more dependent on me. The rest of them are so self-sufficient."

A close relationship between grandfather and grandchild is rare, despite the TV and movie-fed imagery of a buddy-like togetherness that transcends generational differences. Men are less likely to reside with their married children—an uncommon enough circumstance even for women. And men usually don't develop the same casual access of women to their grandchildren through shopping excursions, cooking special foods (Julia Arensberg mentioned her special turkey noodle soup "which my grandchildren love" three times in the course of an interview), babysitting, helping out at parties or in times of sickness. The technical knowledge and the skills that elderly men can impart to today's youth are often outdated.

Yet there are two areas rich with the promise of personal stimulation and shared satisfaction. Grandfathers find their strongest links in common interests in sports or hobbies. They have that rich commodity of time, something that parents, especially fathers, are woefully short of during children's young years. A grandchild is, perhaps, most accessible and most responsive to his grandfather's company between the ages of five and twelve. Earlier he is too diffuse in his energies and physically demanding; older, the child finds himself involved in activities with his peers with whom he is better matched. Grandpa is someone to teach you card games, someone to watch a television sports event with, who will take you fishing once in a while, or go ice skating with you, who knows baseball ratings and helps collect things. Especially responsive are urban, housebound children, though even boys and girls with other children to play with enjoy the opportunity for the warm absorption of someone who gives of himself, who is there for rich, long moments, with whom they do not have to compete or worry about their image. But they chafe at inordinate demands of time and love.

As Grandchildren Grow

As children advance in years, the aura that surrounds the personages of their grandparents begins to dim. Grandparents may not seem as legendary, as competent as they were. Boys and girls begin to notice old-fashioned ways, to be more aware of parents' occasional deprecation of them. Some may begin to think their grandparents funny, but many develop fierce loyalties and are protective of them.

When a relationship with a grandchild has been deeply felt and too heavily relied upon, estrangement during the child's later years can be experienced as a new and grievous loss. For older women especially it can be an assailing development.

Marta Cunningham, a divorcee who raised her blind daughter and her grandchild, was bitter.

"Diedra was a warm, outgoing child; but now she has no time for me. We were once very close. Now

171

I don't always know when she comes home on a weekend from college. I realize there is a large difference between her age and mine; but I have gone through many things and I could help her in some of her problems if she'd let me."

Some find a deepening attachment through the years, recognizing nevertheless a qualitative shift in their relationship. The happiest come to regard the affection of their grandchildren as a dividend, the bonus of a relationship that was its own reward.

It is useless to demand love. In the strategies of aging, grandchildren can bring pleasure along the way. But their dependency is at best brief and sporadic, which is the way it should be. They were never meant to be guides. Nor can the old live vicariously through them; the old have their own lives and their own peer group.

In sum, the post-sixty parent functions best apart from his or her children. A gulf of priorities and interests separate them. This separation is natural and appropriate. Any attempt to reactivate former parent-child dependencies makes for troubled relations and impedes success at the aging game. One may expect an even greater separation from grandchildren, but it doesn't always work that way. Grandchildren may bring, periodically at least, a new basis for enjoyment and communication. Tactically older men and women make the most of relations with their children and grandchildren when they do not, however subtly, seek attention coercively as wronged or deprived or martyred "superkin."

Cy Hart said it: "Basically people get together because they like to be together. What else is there in it for anyone?" The successful old have figured out that this caution extends to their relations with closest kin.

"To whom would it matter a hill of beans if I live or die?" confided Henry Alexander. "I asked myself that."

For this old furniture-maker with a stiff hand, recently widowed and confined after a long period of deepening depression, "Only my brother. That's all," he said. And he remonstrated with himself for not having gone to live with his brother Paul earlier.

"He wanted me to come. A hundred times he said: 'Henry, we've got a big house. The kids are gone. You can come and go as you like.' I should have gone. But I was feeling too blame sorry for myself. And I was worried how his wife would take it."

Two months later when he was released, his brother was there. Henry had gained twenty pounds and his brother teased him. "Pretty soon you'll be as fat as Bessie."

She was a small woman, his brother's wife, and she took Henry's arm and said good-naturedly, "He can't make us mad, can he?"

Six months later, she consented to an interview. "He's a gentle man. You wouldn't know he was there. At first, when my husband talked about it, I wasn't so sure. But we're all getting up there and, well, I had my Mother living with us for ten years, and Paul never complained."

The move to Marin County was for Henry Alexander a return to a region he had known as a child. "At that time, there was nobody but a lot of Irishmen and Italians. No bridge. We took the ferry. We had good times, the lot of us. Went on picnics and dances, and the big thing was the Rose Bowl Pavilion at Larkspur on Saturday nights and the baseball games. I couldn't throw worth a damn. But my brother, Paul, was the star pitcher." And then: "Marin County is great—no smog, sunshine, lots of room."

What was he doing? "Building a barbecue. A big one, wood-trimmed. Have to do something and Paul was never good with his hands. I fix everything that doesn't work. Bessie and I get along fine. She's 100 per cent okay."

The rising influence of brothers and sisters in later life was an unanticipated finding of our study. After sixty, contacts become more frequent than at any other time of life, with the obvious exception of a shared childhood. The renewed sense of empathy is phenomenal. Fully 90 per cent of those we interviewed had living brothers and sisters, and virtually all were able to tell their precise whereabouts, even when widely separated by miles, divergent lifestyles or through early separation.

To the growing number of old who find themselves living alone, the case for siblings is an especially compelling one. The best strategy is often experimental. Brothers and sisters "visit" one another and sometimes these two- or three-week trips develop into prolonged stays. There seems to be not as great a feeling of being a burden (especially to a single person) as with a married son or daughter. Siblings seem to try harder, from a readier base of equality. Being members of the same generation aids communication and reinforces a shared sense of "differentness."

"We talk the same," said Cy Hart, whose sister had just left after a month's visit. "Isn't that funny? I had really forgotten. And I really mean talk *differently*. Eighty years makes a difference in a lot of things. The old expressions, the old-time family jokes that no one else would understand."

It was a curious admission from Cy, who delighted our youngest interviewers with his knowledge of current music, films, and slang.

"It's just plain relaxing. That's all. Perks me up." He gave me one of his conspiratorial glances.

"See what I mean? 'Perks me up.' How often do you hear that these days?"

Travel

For many persons a feeling of restlessness follows retirement: an urge to break through the boundaries that were so long imposed by work and children. Many re-experience drives to explore the farthest reaches of their environment. And this should be encouraged. Travel provides psychological recharging, opens up new vistas of enjoyment, often provides the opportunity for new friendships. Visits to brothers and sisters are often anchoring points on these sometimes extended excursions. Pleasure for its own sake is something most of our interview subjects seemed impelled to disclaim for themselves. Today's old are often cripplingly suspicious of "fun," inexperienced in the association of pleasure with late life, even when they can afford it. Their considerable "Depression Years" heritage may be part of it. Men and women prefer to report it a "duty" to visit one's relatives or something they "had better" do now, if ever. There is an astonishing amount of visiting back and forth, even across great distances. The majority of these with brothers and sisters living outside the state, often in the Midwest and sometimes as far as the East Coast, had seen these relatives within the last five years. Wanderlust is not limited to the wealthy.

A retired nurse, at eighty, had saved for two years to

buy a plane ticket to Chicago and a new outfit so she could go back and visit a sister she hadn't seen in twenty years. Ralph Lawton, with the help of his two married daughters, collected trading stamps for a trip to Hawaii where he could visit with a seventy-year-old sister who is still a Mormon missionary there. And Angelo Alioto, when we last saw him, reported he had found part-time work as a relief bus driver for a local school and was saving these wages toward an eventual trip to the "old country."

For the foreign-born, when retirement, loneliness, or the still strange cultural pressures bear down heavily in old age, it is especially reassuring to think of brothers and sisters still living in the home country. The pull of his native Greece was strong for Apostolos Andromedas, who had fled the state hospital for his skid-row room. He had good friends among other solitary men of the neighborhood—"the gang," and a close attachment with a brother who had immigrated with him fifty years before. But after his brother's death his goal was to return to Greece and the supportive network of a large extended family, especially the home of his only remaining brother.

"Before I die, I am going to see him."

Somehow he saved exactly half of his wages as a waiter in a Howard Street diner. And sixteen months later when we talked for the last time, he had his plane tickets and traveling documents in hand, ready to depart. He had little doubt of his good reception. He was going home again after a long absence. The United States had been a beneficent but strange and sometimes difficult way station.

Moves often bring dramatic uprootings, sometimes in unpredictable ways. Mercedes Miller worked for thirty years in the same, small family-owned gift shop with her husband and later her son. When her husband died she moved into her son's home. However, when life there became difficult, Mrs. Miller escaped by making a trip to see her sister in New York.

"She and her husband live there now with their daughter," she said. "They were wonderful and happy, but they have each other and I felt odd being a third person around, so in a way I was glad to leave." But Mrs. Miller's trip had unexpected dividends.

Doing something different triggered a new, strategically supportive image of herself. "I saw that I was liked for myself. I felt the excitement of having some place to go. I never realized that I could make friends, that people could be *glad* to be with me. It gave me courage." And when she came back:

"I couldn't live that unhappy way anymore. Why, I asked myself, when I don't have to?" She decided it was better, much better to move out of her son's home and into a small apartment of her own. A year later, she reported, "I'll be as honest as I can. Every day isn't wonderful, you know. I miss seeing my grandchildren. But I am happier. And so are they. I plan my days away from the shop and make myself get out and do things. We live in a beautiful city and I have made two new friends."

She has invited her sister and her husband for a visit, "They can have my room and I'll sleep on the sofa. I told them, 'Come. You must. So I can come visit you again.' They will rent a car and we will see California together. I scarcely know it myself."

Movement. Activity. Challenge. Mercedes Miller was, "if not happy, closer to it than I've been in a long, long time. I'm learning."

The experience of Mercedes and others who found stimulation and drive in sometimes dramatic late-life moves suggests a re-examination of the old cautions about radical changes after sixty. When spouses die and friends scatter or die and children find their independent ways, old haunts become just that, haunting shells of happy, active days that are no more. There is a melancholy that attaches to empty rooms and changing streets and diminishing activities.

Some moves present more problems than they solve. But a brother or sister, someone close but not too close, can be the pivot needed at this time for a little safe experimentation. It can have undreamed-of dividends.

Brothers and sisters in their old strengths, and in their new identity as common strategists in the aging game, may find a special sense of investment in one another. There is little lost in the testing. Particularly compelling are trial periods where both candidly explore the pros and cons of a possible life together.

While sibling enmity is sometimes persistent, many men and women report that late life invites a new priority system, a willingness to reactivate precious links to life. It is a time for fence-mending, if it is ever to be done. One woman recalls: "I was walking along Post Street and I saw it in a window: *Raggedy Ann and the Camel with the Wrinkled Knees.* I went in and bought it and mailed it to my brother Ben with a card— 'Remember when I used to read it to you?'" In a week she had a letter from her brother and an invitation to spend the holidays in Arizona.

"I was so glad. We hadn't seen one another in twenty years. And you know, I'd never been out of the state before. It's so much easier and cheaper to travel these days. Gave me itchy feet. Ben wants me to come back to see Spring on the desert. Won't that be something!"

FRIENDS

Even with spouses, brothers and sisters, and grand-children about, each of us needs people we can *choose* to be with, people whose company is sought because we are richer for being with them, with whom we can unwind, and who take us out of our web of ties. Friends please one another; it's no more complicated or portentous than that.

In late life especially, friends bring the world in, and without the preconceived, often loutish prejudices of kin who can take a nervous stand about elderly relatives. Even the kindest can wield cruel cuts in their condescending attention. "My daughter visited me every week, *even if it killed her*. She made that clear," said one woman of sixty-six who finally decided to be less accessible to her immediate family.

"How absurd," she said. "It was hell all the way around. Do they really think we can find pleasure in their little agonies?"

For her and for most, the presence of friends has great bearing upon the enjoyment of life. There is versatility in the challenge and support that friends bring to one another. And friendship can be initiated even in advanced old age—a circumstance that does not hold for dwindling relations based on kinship.

Women are franker than men in expressing their dependency on friends, and their loneliness without them. "I feel actually that I need more friends than ever before," said Nan Buckner. "Really close friends." With her second marriage, Muriel Garner, withdrawing from her long period of depression, made extraordinary efforts to find old friends and to make new ones.

"I used to take friendship for granted as my due," she

says. "Now I have to earn it if I am to have it. I learned that the hard way."

For Amy Peabody, in her strenuous and neurotic resistance to old age, friends are important for reflecting the youthful image she tries to maintain for herself. "People who want to be on the go, that's what I like. As long as I am with people like that I'm all right."

Elderly men rarely are as intense in their expressions of need and are often considerably more passive. Single men, especially those of low socioeconomic status, define friendship most loosely. Frequent but almost superficial contact is prized.

For John Fox, at the age of eighty-three still selling newspapers on a street corner, his customers come to mind when he is asked to name his friends. "When they see me, they say, 'Hi ya, Foxy—think you're gonna live to be a hundred years old?'" Another friend "comes up to see me once a week at the stand." When asked to name the person he feels closest to, he mentions the owner of a nearby jewelry store.

"He likes me," he says. "He'd go to bat for me any time. He comes by the newspaper stand and talks to me all the time."

In the same vein, Hans Weismuller, a long-time widower, speaks of the tenants of the apartment building where he collects rent as his friends.

Married men are still bound up in a pattern of living which allocates social planning to their wives so that they participate, sometimes exclusively, in the activities their wives design for them jointly. But there is latent concern among them about this dependency. And it is validated by their astonishing vulnerability to isolation and mental illness if they lose their wives. Widowers are embarrassed to reveal their isolation, cautious that the absence of friends should not stigmatize them. Even our seemingly invulnerable Jonathan Holt, semi-retired stockbroker, feels sometimes compelled to justify a lack of friends. Others volunteer that they are highly selective, or that they prefer to devote time to other things, or merely that people within their reach do not meet their standards.

Women have greater practice than men in keeping in touch via the telephone or through letter writing. Often they have done this *for* the men through the years. When it becomes critical for men to turn to these aids by themselves, they are apt to lose contact with old friends or be unable to make new ones through their reluctance or discomfort or actual ignorance as to how to keep up friendship.

This is unfortunate. Men, particularly, are thrown on their own resources at a time when they are least equipped to cultivate allies but most in need of them. The old *need* friends. When lost friendships go unreplaced and one ceases to forge new relationships, one's view of the world carries a consensus of the finality of life. Morale lowers. Enthusiasm for life wanes as social withdrawal is intensified. In contrast with mentally healthy men and women, not one psychiatrically hospitalized old person in our survey could point to a close relationship with a friend within a five-year period prior to the onset of symptoms.

Loss of Friendship

Great pride is involved in having held friendship for a long time. It is evidence of one's acknowledged worth in a world where this worth is now suspect. Men and women typically mention associations of ten to twenty or more years. Some are a half-century old.

Replacing friends like these, the old say, is difficult.

Actually it is *impossible*, particularly if men and women are determined to settle only for the same easy intimacy of long-shared reminiscences. But there are other bases for social intercourse. Intimacy does grow once a new attachment is made.

Rationalizations of diminishing contacts are frequent: this diminution is blamed on a decrease in physical energy, a felt inability to reciprocate social invitations, or the breaking of ties with those who have not experienced the same kind of change. Sometimes it is felt that new friends must be limited (if they are developed at all) to those in the same economic status.

Gina Rowles had made calculated breaks with old friends "because my place had grown so shabby. I hated to have people in." Eating out, an expensive undertaking, seems to many to be the only resolution of this problem. In losing their spouses, men especially have also lost their housekeepers and hostesses. "You just don't accept invitations or extend them," says Gene Nathan, the lonely retired salesman whose wife has long been hospitalized.

Older people often feel compelled to restrict their meetings with friends to public places. Problems of transportation sometimes seem insurmountable. Both men and women are reluctant to expose themselves to lengthy trips, requiring mounting and dismounting fast-moving buses and jerky streetcars and transferring to other lines, with long waits, across the city. Night brings the added dangers of crime and violence in the streets.

Any of these developments is unwelcome. None enhances easy friendships. All are real, sometimes grossly threatening problems. The full syndrome is engulfing.

Sad to say, the old often leap to accept the blame for their condition. When Woodrow Karner, a retired engineer whose income was halved on his retirement, says "I can't see anyone because I live less well than I like, or than I used to," he means, in effect, "my condition shames me." *It does not; it shames society.* Or should. But the old compound that shame when they suggest that they deserve no more than they are getting at society's hands, that they are worthless. Some believe it. Susceptibility to such ideas is great when declining social esteem threatens self-esteem. In sometimes morbid introspection the old wrestle with the ethic of their worth. "I have gone through a period of self-evaluation," admitted Mr. Nathan, the retired schoolteacher. "I think I never felt less important to people as a friend than I do right now. I think my desirability as a friend has diminished in the past few years. They see me as a disappointment. They feel sorry for me. They think I could have amounted to more and made more money than I did. And they are right." Devastated by a consensus of his own fabrication, he concludes: "This may be a projection on my part, but I feel they see through my phony dress, the false front that I present to the world. I simply can't be with them anymore." He can almost, but not quite, see the damning effect of his own brutal self-indictment.

Arthur Hopland has drifted into isolation because of a recent accident which left him slightly crippled, though ambulatory, and which cost him his job with the railway. On pension now, he remembers the old days when he "always had good friends." Now he has "no friends, not since I got hurt. We moved. It's not as good a neighborhood. Nobody knows where me and my wife live." Of course he has not told them. He discourages their concern and attention.

Specifically, broad, cumulative changes in living style often brought on by economic downgrading, by illness, or isolation have adversely affected the threshold for friendship—a vital dimension of life after sixty. Many men and women have come to feel personally devalued, unworthy, too shattered, *too old to have friends*. They have drifted into social backwaters almost purposefully. Their present stand (or lack of it) is tactically absurd and adaptively disastrous. It is, rather, the time for a shifting of gears, a reversal of direction, into the mainstream of life.

Some Potential Strategies

Some potential strategies for making friends after sixty can be seen in the life histories of intrepid innovators. Emerging from eight months of institutionalization for acute depression, a resolute widow of sixty-four had this to say. "I shall get an orange crate and two paper cups if I must, and the person who shares them with me will be my friend and I his. Pride is great, but it is not worth that desperate, consuming loneliness."

The remarkable Cy Hart put it this way: "It took me a surprisingly long time to figure it out, for it is really quite simple. It is a matter of pride with almost every older person I know to give more than he receives. But we forget that it isn't always a matter of dollars and cents." The old become so afraid, so insecure about shortchanging one another, about appearing cheap or dowdy *in one another's eyes*, that they sell themselves short or don't extend themselves at all. "There are so many of us," he continued, "drifting around in our respective loneliness. We should have greater fear of what we fail to give than of what we may take too much of." Americans are too used to keeping score.

If the problems of late life are detached from bruised

egos, the urgent business of resolving these problems can get under way. "I plan at least a week ahead," said one woman, "and I've worked out a kind of formula which I try to stick to. I must *go* somewhere with someone or to someone's home once a week, and I must have someone *in* once a week. Once a month I arrange to do something I've never done before or go to some place I have not seen in a long time." She is a seventy-year-old pensioner, walks with a cane because of an arthritic condition, and has a yearly income of just under $4,800. This is augmented once in a while with small money gifts from her two daughters. "I used to discourage them, but I don't anymore. I said to them, 'It will do more than Christmas or birthday gifts to keep me on my own and that's good for both of us!' " Her two-room apartment is on busy Polk Street in San Francisco over a launderette. "I used to live out in the Sunset district. At night you might as well be in a box. Buses every hour and streets black as ink."

In her small kitchenette she prepares "something at least once a week for a guest. You'd be surprised what I can turn out." Most old people alone are weary of the cafeteria and cheap restaurant escapes and enjoy the simplest home fare. "A thick minestrone soup, an omelet, and I can still bake a good pie. I've done it all for under $5.00." Sometimes she simply serves coffee and homemade cookies.

Ralph Lawton at sixty-six had "never stirred a pot in my life. It was a matter of pride." When his wife died he took his meals either in his son-in-law's home or a restaurant. "I was with them or I was alone. A colossal nuisance and bored stiff. It dawned on me finally how God-damned helpless I was." He had a small savings reserve and five hundred dollars left from his wife's insurance. Something he had always wanted to do was take a sea trip to Alaska, and he decided to take advantage of the off-season rates and do just that. "What better time? But I couldn't get a cabin to myself. The steamship company uses computers to match you up with someone and they put me in with a fellow from the Bay Area. Little younger than me. We hit it off. He used to work for a lumber outfit up near Juneau, and was going back for a visit. I really saw the North."

They returned to San Francisco with pledges of continued friendship. "It was a kind of turning point for me," Ralph said. "And in a way I knew it. You know, I was kind of panicky though. He was a travel buff and I knew he lived pretty well."

The lumberman's standard of living *is* superior to Ralph's but it has not deterred regular visits between them. "We go out for a couple of beers, or once in a while go to a ball game." And through this more active man he has made new acquaintances. As a guest at meetings of a travel club to which his friend belongs, he has grown more comfortable in casual interchanges. "There are some married couples too, and I have been invited twice to their homes." Six months before our last interview, Ralph Lawton had taken the plunge as host.

"When Irene, my wife, was alive we used to have people over. The house is full of all the stuff you need. Not elaborate, but it's there—plenty of glasses, cups, ashtrays, dishes." His daughter helped him. "No big deal," he said. "One of those National Geographic specials on TV. We all wanted to see it. There was my friend, two couples, and a fellow I have not seen since I quit work—I called him on an impulse. We had some beer and then watched the show and then my daughter served some coffee and cake. I was nervous, but I'm glad I did it."

Social planning has become more natural for him. "Next week we are going to go on a Bay cruise. In the middle of the week there's not so much of a crowd and it's cheaper." He has mastered enough of the kitchen "to be able to fry an egg or heat soup or broil a hamburger. And one of these days I am going to have a go at some of that foreign cooking these travel nuts are always raving about. Maybe have them all over. I don't worry so much about flubbing anymore and I prepare what I can afford."

People alone sometimes find it worth the risk to experiment with joint living arrangements with a friend. The camaraderie of a South-of-Market Irishman with Whitey, a part-time watchman he met when both were hospitalized for heart conditions, resulted in a new pattern for both. Through the efforts of hospital personnel they found a small garden-apartment in the Potrero Heights district where the Irishman's social security and Whitey's limited paychecks go further on a shared budget. Whitey is a good cook, and the Irishman contributes his share in handy-work around their place and in the neighborhood for a little extra money. They both like to fish in San Francisco Bay and Whitey works in the small garden.

Some new friendships are happily made with considerably younger individuals. This is possibly a reflection of the older person's need sometimes for someone better capable of handling the environment, but it also mirrors the negative image some of the old create for themselves as potential friends. "I'm not too anxious to mingle with people my age," says a seventy-two-year-old widow. "They just talk about aches and pains. I feel I can't learn anything from them."

Ralph Lawton, the Alaska traveller, speaking of a

woman of his age with whom he had been paired off at a church breakfast, ventured: "I really wanted to be friendly, but she moaned about everything from the sermon to the food."

At any age, a dour attitude and bleak expectations are unappealing socially; in old age they alienate the very people who can dissipate them. "At sixty," says one man, "who needs these prophets of doom?" At eighty, even less. It does not win friends, however tempting the posture.

In the criteria for friendship put forth by many in our study, stress was laid upon two qualities: accessibility and worthwhile personality traits. A friend is someone you can get to, be with, who makes an effort to meet you halfway, who will visit with you, respond to your need for talk, diversion, change, incorporation, novelty of experience (a universal psychic need even into extreme old age). And these are regarded as reciprocal commitments, replacing in late life the posture of dominance often sought in earlier relationships. Defensiveness, the suggestion of personal advantage, a calculated bid for some level of social control—these alienate friends in late life. In terms of personality, a friend should be amiable, interesting, not bossy, congenial, good company, stimulating but someone you can feel at ease with, a regular guy. Elaborate clothes and housing are more often frightening than enticing.

In the aging game, the old are too often like blindfolded players exploring the recesses of dark and empty rooms. That is not where the action is and not the way to find it. You can age successfully without friends, especially where marital ties remain close and supportive and one's children empathetic, but it's harder.

Even lifetime loners find themselves facing a newly perilous equation: one against all. No, the battle for success and sanity after sixty is not intelligently fought without all the alliances one can get.

The older man or woman who does not maintain friends and self-consciously substitutes for lost ones by all the strategy at his or her command is functioning with less than the full potential of social armature. In the rigged contest of the aging game it is an absurd concession.

GROUPS

The activities planned by organizations are not as important to old people as the opportunity to interact with others in a convivial setting. A free, easy-going atmosphere, suitable for informal conversation, is more appreciated than high-powered programs for self-improvement or social service. What brings older men and women to meetings is rather the implicit desire to remain within the flow of humanity, still interested, creative and alive.

Multi-age groups keep the old in touch with people of all ages and provide them first-hand knowledge of culture change and the values that change with it. Informal exchange of this kind also reaffirms the logic of their continuing incorporation in society, softening the natural conflicts between generations. Often older members find that their added years actually bring dividends to the group in mediating skills, historical knowledge, grace and perspective, and the luxury of free time.

Unhappy old people characteristically dwell on the damning effect of age on any kind of collective involvement. They consistently fail to perceive opportunities for substitutive sources of pride, personal development, and satisfaction. Often one catches an uneasiness about social contacts in general.

"I don't like groups of women. They are too catty, just gossipy," said Rena Baronian. "Besides, you never know with strangers what you're getting into."

Miss Peabody, still in full flight from old age, recalled how she joined the Rebecca Lodge in her early twenties but was always an indifferent member. When young, she disliked having so many members older than she. Now, ironically, she resists identification with them, "rubbing elbows with women who are older than I am, like I will be."

A retired schoolteacher, struggling with loneliness and despair, explained his growing inactivity in the American Legion. "I don't have to go down there anymore and listen to them tell me a lot of stuff that I already know about politics. Besides, who listens to an old man?"

Organizational membership is not a last-chance depot for those without human companionship. Actually, it more typically is the other way around. Those most devoid of social contacts rarely turn to clubs to seek them out. They don't know how. Those who are already involved become more so through group affiliation.

Janet Bennington does not lack friends and relatives, but derives the greatest satisfaction from her continued involvement with the Retired Nurses Association. Within it a certain prestige adheres to seniority. She is eighty-three and speaks with pride of her thirteen years as "chaplain" (an official post) of this association.

"In that way, I'm kept busy. I get on the bus to visit

these sick nurses at army hospitals as well as at the old-age home for nurses, and the association pays my traveling expenses. Sometimes, when they see me scurrying around, they perk up . . . wonder why they lie there feeling so glum and sorry for themselves."

Eric Jespersen, whose membership in the Socialist Labor Party dates from the 1920s, finds now it does much to provide him not only with activity, but with a continuing ideology and purpose in life. "Although the party is still small," he explains, "we are a pretty active group. We meet more than twice a month sometimes, and we all do what we can. Like me. I distribute the Socialist newspaper to the Geary Street district. Speak to a lot of people."

What To Join

What specifically should persons who are over sixty join? How do they become involved, particularly if they have had little practice in it? Are clubs exclusively geared to the old good or bad bets in terms of successful aging?

Few men and women in our study group had any idea of the wide range of organizations available to them on both a national and strictly local level. Some who thought they *might* be interested could never get over the initial hurdle of making contact with an appropriate group.

Some had had the experience of going alone to a sterile hall to sit in isolated discomfort throughout the long rituals of some great fraternal organization. "I'm not sure what was going on exactly. Election of officers, I think. The big thing was something about the duties of the sergeant-at-arms and there was a lot of gavel banging." In narrating his impressions of that evening, this sixty-four-year-old man seemed to have total recall. "I came in a little late and sat in the back of the room on this folding chair in an almost empty row. Up front all the seats were taken. Halfway through, this woman came back and said could she help me? and I said I used to belong and wanted to see what was going on. She was very nice and said to be sure to stay until the meeting was over and I could have some refreshments and meet people." But he didn't stay. "It was boring as hell and by ten o'clock I decided to sneak out and catch my bus. It was way out to hell and gone anyway. I never went back. Hell, I outgrew that stuff when I was twenty. I remembered. I hadn't liked it any better then, either."

A few thrive on this kind of ritual activity. But they have long experience with survival in these environments. "I was past-president of the woman's auxiliary of my union and treasurer of the state's largest garden club. In May I organized the annual luncheon. We had the biggest turnout ever. When you have been in it as long as I have, you know just what to order and how to get things done. It's very demanding."

New or second-time-around joiners have most success when they: (1) stay as close to their residential areas as they can; and (2) look for small groups with explicit interests—card or chess groups, folk dancers, hospital auxiliaries, drama companies, religious, charitable, or public-action groups attached to a local church or headquarters. It is good policy to learn the name of someone who will be there to whom one can present oneself *before the meeting begins.*

Staying relatively close to home makes attendance less of a big deal. It makes going out more feasible even in inclement weather, and contacts are more easily made with people one can see again. Also, these small local groups will generally go to some effort to see that men and women have rides home—and possibly to the next get-together. That's helpful and it all enhances the personal dimension of social exchange. More informal conversation, more exploration of common interests.

Neighborhood newspapers are often great sources of information about group activities. Sometimes just the realization that someone is interested will bring invitations, but people have to know you are around. Find out from a friend what she or he has found to do, ask your pastor (and be prepared to be put to work), find out if your local school could use your skills. Or, as Maude said: "Go ahead and speak to a neighbor; the worse that can happen is a rebuff."

Ralph Lawton, who now enjoys golf as well as travel, found out about a small public club he hadn't known existed, just a half-mile from his home, simply by confessing to the woman who lives next door (with whom he had only nodding acquaintance) that he wanted something new to do. For one dollar he can play peewee golf, or hit a bucket of balls off a small driving range. And there's always someone who will play the small nine-hole course with him.

No one's social activity should be limited to exclusively male or female or old-age clubs. Such concentration of resources is bad. It is atomistic, distancing. It further fractures the break between men and women, between the old and the rest of society. The old need to build up faith in the potential rewards of being a full part of the social scene, of acting with their fellows as still interesting, vital men and women, as good companions.

In the United States today that means the old themselves will have to create these rewards and these opportunities for incorporation. The old have greater opportunity inside groups than outside them to achieve their personal desires and to improve the social capacity of this nation to provide a richer dimension of life for *all* its members.

III

A REVISED GAME PLAN: CREATING NEW GUIDELINES

Successful aging is a product of the five distinctive tactics that we have discussed. If you meet the challenges involved in each, you will age successfully; if you do not, you cannot. The aging game will only tenuously be won, however, if all these efforts do not contribute to a new national image of aging and more rewarding goals for every older American.

This final challenge, a new game plan for successful aging in the United States today, builds on the challenges that precede it. It is facilitated by them. It translates a new image of the self, a new life stance, and a developing strategy for satisfaction and success in late life into a program of action. A confrontation of culture.

The creation of new cultural norms for life after sixty is long overdue in the United States. Such new norms, built on a premise of worth and humanity, are critical to the health and happiness of a ninth of our population (a rapidly growing percentage). However, if they are to come at all, it will be through the initiative of the old themselves. Through their creative living.

The ability of some men and women to act creatively lies in a healthy mixture of skepticism with regard to established dogma and a naive approach toward the most daring hypotheses. The creative are not disdainful of the current order of things; they are rather oblivious that any sanctity attaches to it. The way things are is not necessarily, except by default, the way things ought to be.

Exploratory drive and creativity appear natural to human beings. Children are un-self-consciously creative until we teach them to prize the mundane and familiar. For the drive to act creatively is a perishable commodity. It needs, eventually, a receptive society if it is to be sustained without peril. Society does not much like creators. They disturb the present order of things and the complacency that goes with it. But the old may have a special edge on creativity. They can regard the established order as suspect all the more since they are being eased, in any case, from its strictures. There is little peril in rocking the boat if you are going to be dumped in the deep anyway. Society's studious efforts to disengage the old can actually be their passport to freedom, *if* they learn to manipulate society's "planlessness" for the old to their advantage.

The rub comes in society's discouragement of the very attitudes and actions that would facilitate innovation by the old. To them we preach the inappropriateness of ingenuity, courage, imagination, and skepticism about the established order. Rather, we tell them that resignation, humility, and self-centeredness are appropriate attitudes. And we reward these personality characteristics among the old. We say, you may find stagnation difficult at first, but it is good for you. And society promises to compensate with affectionate nurturing. This, we assure them, will fill the void of inactivity. It is our culture's primary gesture toward a code of behavior.

The danger is not only that the aged are prohibited from creative activity but that society's tactics will insure that eventually they are rendered incapable of any activity, psychically as well as socially incapacitated. For with a sure insidiousness society renders impotent its post-sixty population if it can, and then isolates them on the basis of their condition—their age-linked condition. Those who survive the ordeal are regarded as eccentrics or geniuses. And many are just that. They must possess unusual ego-strength to disavow society's assessment of them.

Increasingly, older men and women are attracted either to communities exclusively designed for them, as in the euphemistically called "adult-living communities," or to settings such as mobile-home parks where less affluent retired individuals congregate. In both types of settings retired people build lifestyles around leisure pursuits rather than work.

Ignoring old age by emphasizing a cult of pseudo-activity created within the communities seems to work for some people, providing the basis for a healthy self-image and insulating them against disquieting changes on the outside. The fundamental source of appeal, however, writes anthropologist Susan Byrne of Arden, her pseudonym for a wealthy California retirement community, "lies in its provision of an environment that permits residents to live much as they did in earlier years." For some people adaptation in these high-density, age-segregated communities apparently requires less drastic behavior modification than growing old in the urban or suburban areas from which they have come. But few men and women escape the insidious reminders that golden-age worlds are at best a compromise refuge from a society that has little regard for them.

The old are in much the same position today as women were at the turn of the century. Men set legal norms, controlled political and economic action, and had the vote. Women were first absurd and then a threat in their bid for recognition. Society today means the young (actually the non-old) who control these things, and the old are not even seen as absurd or threatening; nobody knows they're there. (Almost nobody. An unfortunate few are charged with keeping them out of sight and mind.) What the old must do today is what women did then. Women used not so much the vote as a new ebullient consciousness of their potential to free themselves from unexamined social restraints. With ripe confidence they become a force to be reckoned with, so that they were accommodated in the life of our nation *as women*.

Political consciousness is not highly developed among the elderly. They will vote for a candidate who promises to do something for them, something explicit, particularly at a local level: special transportation discounts, tax benefits, increased insurance protection, cheaper housing. But until recently, with the successes of such groups as the militant Gray Panthers and the sizable National Retired Teachers Association, rarely have they banded together to accomplish their most modest goals. It is not that they resist this form of action; it is rather that it does not seem to occur to them. The prospect of success in some joint endeavor apparently is so remote a consideration that the endeavor can't get off the ground.

On one occasion when I showed an ex-stevedore a

newspaper article about the success of a group of retirement-community residents in using the courts jointly to thwart plans for a freeway that would have demolished their homes, he replied: "Probably never intended it in the first place." I showed the same article to a woman of sixty-five. "You can't believe what they put in the papers," she said. It was like a projective test. Another man said, "Bet some smart lawyer used them as a front group." And again. "That'll be the day. They gotta go slow if the papers get on to them. Soon as it dies down, they'll put 'em on the street and you'll never hear a word about it."

To these elderly, maximizing their strength is, as one fellow put it, "like piling up flab—you'll never make muscle out of it." While one American in fifty belongs to a political club (scarcely a smashing display of democratic activism in itself), the figure dips to one in two hundred for the post-sixty man or woman. The old are not given to political involvement, not realizing that by their simple presence they have had influence on welfare legislation and social reforms. In a country where 5 per cent of the vote usually decides the election, 17 per cent (the post-sixty voting population) could have dramatic effect.

A sure, strong realization that change can come, with richly overdue dividends not only for the individual but for the culture, is a powerful stimulus to innovation, to creativity on the social scene.

Two Options for Success After Sixty

Right now in the United States only limited ways exist of living successfully though sixty or over. One way lies in the manipulation of major values of our culture: productivity, change, novelty of experience, independence, material gain, and the drive for recognition. The second way involves judicious investment in currently minor themes (secondary or lower-keyed values of American life): conservation instead of exploitation, self-acceptance instead of the sustained struggle for advancement, congeniality, cooperation, love and concern rather than control of others. Despite considerable lip service, these are less popular goals of our culture. Either they are only intermittently pursued by the bulk of the people, or they have a smaller, less influential following.

For older Americans both options are perilous, but for different reasons. They are denied all but tangential access to the former, and success in the latter is generally denigrated. But some skill in facing both challenges is critical to successful aging since together they constitute the existing blueprint for living within our culture.

What is involved throughout is really a very basic kind of coping. Coping is the individual's ability to manage both the demands of his environment and his particular personal tensions—needs, or stresses in psychological terms. We all learn to cope. We must. Or we should be too vulnerable to live. Our culture teaches us how to cope. From birth we are indoctrinated into techniques for survival in our culture. We learn formulas for success, even though under certain circumstances the goals may be untenable. Some goals are more widely sought than others and we accept actions geared to their attainment as natural, really too normal to be called laudable. We understand and empathize with people who appear well directed toward these goals because that's where we are headed too.

From early life we are geared to success. It is a national characteristic to be challenged by obstacles, but we are demolished by failure, which we regard as testimony of personal unworthiness. The past holds no interest for us except as a foil to the present; it allows us to point triumphantly to how far we have come. We measure progress in dollars and cents, accumulated wealth, and power symbols, *not* in moral enrichment or grace or personal maturity. Defense of the latter, especially in the absence of the former, suggests a contrived rationale for second-best performance. Introspective skills are simply not our cultural cup of tea, though philosophers and poets (but not usually old ones) may command considerable public adulation.

The pattern of life in the United States today is built upon a consensus of what is or is not worth doing or worth striving for. These are the values of a culture, and the old, like other age groups, are subject to them. In their studies of traditional cultures, anthropologists have often argued that the old are more valued and better accommodated than in technologically advanced societies such as ours. Writing of his childhood in Mongolia, Onon writes that: "According to the thinking of our people, honors and riches are bestowed by mere men, but ripe old age is a gift from Heaven." As a consequence no one makes any attempt to conceal advancing years. "On the contrary, all could look forward to that golden autumn period of life when, full of years and rich experiences of living, they would receive that special respect and consideration which would be their greatest reward." Of course, few people lived to reach that golden period.

Sociologist Irving Rosow has argued an inverse relationship between economic affluence and a cultural ethic of the worth of the aged. That is, the better the economic picture the less valued the elderly, and the worse the economic status the more positive the ethic of their social worth. This correlation certainly holds in impoverished countries such as India, Mexico, and in much of Africa and South America, under conditions where all hands are valued in tending to field and animals, or in cooking and in caring for small children. The old are encouraged to contribute to family and village activities for as long as they can and they are valued for their contributions. In nonliterate cultures especially, the old are walking repositories of knowledge, and are often highly regarded as decision-makers in religious, marital, and political affairs.

Although some accounts of life in the non-Western world may have overdrawn the picture of respect accorded the aged, it does seem clear that old people in these countries who continue to show interest in and participate in community activities are highly regarded. In the Indian and peasant villages of Spanish America, for example, George Foster has shown how, through continuing service to the community, an individual may achieve the status of "principal," or distinguished elder—rich in merit and prestige, no longer ambitious for world rewards. It is difficult to argue that in our affluent culture the old are accorded comparable opportunities for respect, community involvement, and self-actualization. The ability to match action to socially approved goals is inversely related to advancing age in the United States today. As it is, *right now*, the old either can *not* act toward socially approved goals, *or* can act *only* toward goals that enjoy no social endorsement, or at best low-level support.

The old can change this. Only the old, in fact. For the one in nine Americans now sixty-five or over, the one in seven who is sixty, and the millions more who will be in those brackets one day, successful aging demands that dominant American values be stripped of youth priorities, and secondary values of their old-age identification. The guidelines are clear: first, enlarge opportunities for continuing involvement of older men and women in the major values of the culture; second, intensify social commitment to presently minor values (more congenial to the old) on the part of other age groups.

Stay With the Action

Much of the problem is tactical: keeping the unwanted old where the action is, returning atrophying spectators to the live scene. American culture defines mental health as social involvement and it has come to be that. Noninvolvement and inactivity cause physical and mental illness.

To join the action or stay with it, you must know what is going on. You have to play by the established rules, or at least know them well enough to evade them to your advantage. It's all a kind of game, though the analogy can be pushed too far. American life is complicated and the players are many. Benched players, such as the old, are frightfully visible and expendable. But the strategy holds. Personal stature, though you are old, is greatest when you advance the culture toward its designated goals; it is least when you impede it or even seem to impede it. You can change the rules of action only by identifying with the game. Survival lies with the action, with success in using it to your advantage.

Let me put it in a different context. I am thinking of the time I stopped off in Hong Kong on my way to fieldwork in India. My arrival could not have been more badly timed. The political climate had been smolderingly anti-American for weeks and the day my plane landed three Americans were badly mauled on a downtown street. For my part, I hadn't an inkling of trouble. I had come to Hong Kong from rural Japan and had not seen a newspaper or heard a radio broadcast in English in days. My hotel was in a rather rundown section of Kowloon, far from the tourist havens of Victoria Island. After I'd unpacked I put on a pair of slacks, tied back my hair, and went out in the crowded streets. Kowloon takes some getting used to. It is impossible simply to take a walk. The sidewalks are a moving mass of humanity and locomotion is a matter of allowing oneself to be moved along in the general flow of bodies. When you want to cross a street or turn a corner you must work your way gradually to the fringe of the sidewalk and become incorporated in that mass which is veering toward your destination.

I had dinner many blocks from my hotel in a near-deserted restaurant, lured by the sound of American music. The small radio was perched near the cashier's cage and it was as I was paying my check that I heard the news broadcast cautioning Americans to stay off the streets. I hadn't seen a cab anywhere and I began the long trek back to my hotel feeling uncomfortably like history in the making. I was glad I was in slacks. The other women were in slacks. Or were they? As I turned to look about me, a realization hit me. We were so close, all of us, so pushed together that we couldn't *see* one another. *They* could have no more accurate impression of me than I of *them*. They didn't have the least idea what or who I was.

It was after ten o'clock and some of the shop lights were going out. Here and there the sidestreets were darkening and all of a sudden it seemed strange to me that where I was there should still be such a concentration of bodies. For some reason I looked up, and there above me and behind me and to the right and left of me were banners and placards and bright streamers. The

204

noise took on a new sound, that of chanting, and as we surged around a corner I saw on one of the posters the body of Uncle Sam crushed beneath a fire-breathing dragon. My knees went liquid for a minute. I knew where I was. I was in the middle of an anti-American demonstration!

My mind was churning, but I moved on, was propelled on. After a while I began to think, "I hope we meet no Americans. I hope there are no Americans on the streets." It was a prayer that did not consciously include me. My identity at that time lay with a different group. In a very real sense I was a part of that group. My safety lay in that continued identification, and so long as it was not ruptured I was safer than I would have been outside it, than I would have been anywhere on Kowloon. I was a part of the action. And my legs moved me resolutely along. A block from my hotel I recognized a landmark, a billboard with a "Permapress" shirt below a blaze of Chinese script. By the time we got abreast of the lobby I had sidled to the edge of the group and slipped quickly inside the building.

An electrifying feeling stayed with me a long time, not so much of fear (unbelievably that passed) but of challenge. I had the tremulous but strangely exhilarating realization that I had come through it all unscathed because safety lay in the last place I would have looked: the eye of the hurricane. And I had used it to my advantage.

The whole swelling tide of modern life is a challenge for the older person. It is unpleasant and misdirected sometimes, but participation is exhilarating and life-giving. You move out or you are moved out of it at your peril. Strategy begins within it. Success and sanity lie in involvement.

Few of the major values of American life are advan-

tageous to the old or facilitate their successful adaptation. That's too bad. That should be changed. But as old
Cy Hart said, "Nobody promised roses." It's the way
things are just now.

The conditions that vex our old people are the flesh
and blood of our society. Work, money, autonomy, sexuality: these are the banners of the parade. Success in
late life is predicated less upon distinction in these than
it is upon simple identification with them. Distinction
is delightful and further insurance. But it is not critical.

This is what the old do not seem to know. Instead of
succumbing with docility and confusion and fear to a
"process of disengagement," the post-sixty should be
busy charting their own "process of re-engagement."
And they should be absorbed in it as though their lives
depended on it. Their social lives most certainly do;
their physical and psychic lives, more than they know.
When you are sixty it is sour grapes to deplore the pace
of American life, its drive and self-absorption, the
tyranny of work and money, the mirage of autonomy,
and the labored pervasiveness of sex on the contemporary scene. If sixty brings new insights that
seriously bring these values into challenge, there
is more danger than advantage in airing them. If they
are bouncing you from the establishment, groans
and epithets are to be expected. Your wounded cries
and recriminations do not come under the heading of
philosophy. They confirm your vulnerability and
bitterness. There is little conviction in disdain for
work when you have just been arbitrarily retired. And
the mother or mother-in-law with no place to go is not a
privileged house guest.

The process of re-engagement would guard the vital
links to social life that remain to the old and build upon
them. Rather than viewing old age as an inevitable

mutual withdrawal on the part of the individual and society (the theory of disengagement), re-engagement sees it as a point of inevitable redefinition based on mutual involvement. Formal definitions of old age, of the appropriate time for retirement, for desexing, for dependency would have to yield to functional assessments based on a particular man or woman's continuing capacity for stimulating social and physical identification with the world around him or her.

The old cannot surrender their right to work if they are able, to control their money, to live decently, and to love whom they wish. At forty or fifty society respects the individual's right to guard from usurpation these prerequisites to the pursuit of happiness. What dissipation of logic makes defensible, and even normative, their destruction at sixty? The old should view these as theirs rightfully and not settle for less.

The Guidelines of Change

But they must make their stand as a new breed, a new social group, and from a posture of pride. *Then* will they be able to speak and be heard and remind America of what she already suspects. Not only that the old are more durable than it is convenient for society to admit, but that they identify other rich and promising goals of human endeavor that the United States now most urgently needs to consider and explore, goals in whose attainment advanced age offers special advantage.

The United States revels still in an image of itself as young. A young, strong, upstart nation that made an old world take notice. Depending on your authority we are a nation of conformists or individualists, work-driven or fun-absorbed, aggressive or intrinsically benevolent, uptight or hang-loose, the most enlightened or the most decadent culture in the world. Or we're all of these, the most schizoid collection of bodies culturally assembled in the history of man's long existence.

On one thing all authorities agree. We are driven. Ideologically as well as technologically what we espouse we do with a national zest that, to some writers at least, is suggestive of mass pathology. And we delight in running innovation into obsolescence at record-shattering speeds.

The truth is that the United States as a country is having aging problems of its own. That the qualities of acquisitiveness and exploitation which fired and sustained its early growth may now, *should* now, legitimately be tempered with other values more appropriate to its present status is a consideration not easily accepted. Despite the signs of excess—mounting inflation, ecological devastation, restless youth, angry minorities—the United States remains more defiantly, thrashingly, persistently younger than ever. And it defends, more destructively than any mental patient, its own sick condition. Conservation, contemplation, and concern for others rather than control of them, these values that distinguish maturity, are far yet from being core values of American culture. They are, however, those in whose development and dissemination the old have special empathy and practice. Though they do not yet realize it, our older Americans are a very important part of our national human resources and can contribute to the enrichment, so urgently needed, of the quality of America's national life.

Those who survive best in the late years of life are simply those who have been able, at their own pace, eventually to merge their pursuits of the primary values of our culture with some alternative values that have been around all along. Values through which they have

208

singular opportunity to find satisfaction and to point the way for new dimensions of personal and social growth. The problems of the aged merely dramatize problems that *exist in less-aggravated form for the entire adult population.*

As a people, we have lost the sense of wholeness of our world, of the logical fit of generations with one another, of the rhythm of taxing work and replenishing rest, of the expectable distance between dreams and reality, goals and achievement, of discrimination between freedom from want and insatiable desire.

"The people who have grown up since World War II," said Margaret Mead, "have been bombarded by all the fragmented things in the world, and have never experienced a whole culture. They are overcome by it too early, so that they never learn to sense the holistic quality, the pattern within the diversity of a social system." We live today too close to the canvas of life. So distracted by the strip before us that we never see the total picture. We pick acquisitively at the bright things— money, stimulation, recognition, and power.

The old live with different images, born of a different past, a different cultural heritage. And while our present world would profit from an occasional look backward, from a sense of heritage, the elderly won't. Not right now. Given the present cultural equation they must see first to their survival. That means learning to adapt *now* to the given pace, a given set of priorities. I do not mean they should embrace these, but that they should learn to use them to their own advantage. And the way they adapt will set models for all of us when we are in their place.

Fortunately for the old and for all of us, cultures change. When life becomes unbearably ugly or perilous or dull, we are reminded that we ourselves have shaped this destiny. We consider other patterns of living. Today in the United States we are seeing the surging signs of change, a mounting impatience with the outmoded values that are destroying us ecologically, socially, and personally. We appraise with new wonder and an alien respect the delicate balance that links us all in culture as in nature. Change will come. No doubt about it.

But in the meantime I don't think it is paranoid for the old to consider everyone under sixty the enemy when everyone under sixty *is* the enemy. You can scarcely be a guide if they won't let you out of the tent. The young themselves make it clear. Their credo has been: don't trust anyone over thirty. They say it and mean it and are inheriting the earth. The old must say and mean: don't trust anyone *under sixty*. And aspire to a better corner of that earth. There is a way.

IV

PUTTING IT ALL TOGETHER: WINNING THE AGING GAME

The formula for successful aging which this book has set forth is one which 1,200 post-sixty men and women helped to shape. And it works.

Successful aging is a matter of confrontation and action. Confrontation is with the self and with a culture that prescribes social death and psychic decay for men and women who are guilty of survival after sixty. Action means full-scale cultural combat in a rigged and perilous universe. The goal is a new personal and social equation in late life. There is no substitute for this struggle. And it can be won.

The five tactics of successful aging have no inherent magic. What they do is to outline a course, not only of survival, but of strategically sound progress to happiness and status today after sixty. They are a way of coping with oneself and with the world as an old person. *An old person*. That is where the magic lies. The special magic of continued life, not nascent death. A new pride, a new identity, a new and rational place in

211

the scheme of things, as potentially happy and significant as anyone, simply older.

The tactics of aging are eminently worthy of our best efforts. If the old can only allow expression of them to themselves, their secret selves, these challenges will furnish their own impetus to action.

ONE: *Accept yourself as old*. You haven't an alternative really.

TWO: *Develop a clear perspective on late life*. Old age may not be your idea of the most glorious development, but it has happened and you have now to decide what to do with it. One to two decades of life remain. Maybe more. It is inglorious and mad and a sellout to chart of them a personal agony. That's society's blueprint. To admit of an alternative possibility, a blueprint for happiness, though old, sets the stage for successful aging.

THREE: *Replace lost satisfactions*. Learn to substitute. Look to what you have, not to what you have lost. Make the most of every resource you have. Study yourself, your strengths and weaknesses. Study society's strengths and weaknesses. Compensate where the attrition of resources is inhibiting. Adapt or innovate lifestyles compatible with your goal of successful aging.

FOUR: *Develop the resources that count*. Think money, health, and love. Master the specific strategies that will get you from where you are to where you want to be.

FIVE: *Develop the alliances that count*. Think allies, and always, always, think action and involvement.

In the aging game success is dependent on a calculated program of resistance to society's planned disengagement of its old.

Finally, mold a new rich life for yourself and help to

achieve the same for others—a revised game plan for aging. Use the major values of the culture to stay with the action, but lose no opportunity to further social support of those secondary values that will enhance the special potential of the older American and improve our society. Be instrumental in the creation of new guidelines for aging.

In other words, *confront your culture*. As Cy Hart said, "Nobody promised roses," but the rewards are impressive: success, sanity, and sex after sixty.

Notes

PREFACE

A full description of the methodology, testing instruments, and major findings of the research on which this book is based appeared in *Culture and Aging: An Anthropological Study of Older Americans* (Margaret Clark and Barbara Gallatin Anderson. Springfield, Ill.: Charles C. Thomas, Pub., 1967). Our research identified what we then called the "tasks" of aging, adaptations to be made as one grows older. I later regretted the "task" designation, which made aging sound like hard work and no fun at all. Also, the term seemed to distort the actual challenge of aging. In *The Aging Game* I have rethought, reinterpreted, and enlarged upon earlier ideas to develop a tactical approach to creating a successful old age.

Jules Henry's *Culture Against Man* is worth reading (New York: Random House, 1965). His chapter on human obsolescence is one of the most chilling indictments ever written of the indignities suffered by the old.

INTRODUCTION

The statistical data on aging used in this book are drawn almost exclusively from *Developments in Aging*, the annual reports of the United States Senate, Special Committee on Aging. These publications can be obtained from the United States Government Printing Office, Washington, D.C., for a modest charge, or at your local library. Two volumes are published annually: you will probably want Part I only, unless you have a keen interest in the appendixes in Part II. These regular reports constitute the continuing study, authorized by the Senate "of any and all matters pertaining to problems and opportunities of older people, including, but not limited to, problems and opportunities of maintaining health, of assuring adequate income, of finding employment, or engaging in productive and rewarding activity, of securing proper housing, and when necessary, of obtaining care and assistance." Findings and recommendations of a host of public and private agencies, foundations, and clubs are included in the reports. Much of it is fascinating reading, but there are also tedious and overcomprehensive sections. A detailed table of contents helps you through the morass of data.

I THE ODDS AND THE CHALLENGE

Amy Peabody, Angelo Alioto, and Maude, like all the persons in this book, are real people—men and women I came to know in the course of my research. Although I have changed their names and disguised information that might otherwise identify them, the accounts of their actual lives and personalities certainly required no embellishment by me. From the beginning of my work with the old I have been struck by the way many people become increasingly individualistic as they age. In too much of the literature on aging the old are made to seem all of a piece, all alike, as if late life is a kind of "cloning process." Nothing could be further from the truth. I hope the pages I've devoted to them do some justice to the rich variations in character among them.

"Older Americans: Facts and Potential," by Judith Murphy and Carol Florio (in *The New Old: Struggling for Decent Aging*, edited by Ronald Gross, Beatrice Gross, and Sylvia Seidman. Garden City, N.Y.: Doubleday, 1978) provides an illuminating statistical profile of older Americans. Murphy and Florio also summarize a 1974 Harris poll conducted for The National Council on the Aging, the most extensive survey of attitudes on aging (among all age groups) ever conducted in the United States.

II THE STRATEGY OF AGING

Tactic Two: Develop a Clear Perspective on Late Life

The comments of Florida Scott-Maxwell are from a lecture first delivered on the Third Programme of the British Broadcasting Corporation. This sensitive and witty personal account of aging was reproduced in the BBC's publication, *The Listener* (October 14, 1954, pp. 627–629). I have never understood why it is not more widely circulated, especially in gerontological literature.

TACTIC THREE: REPLACE LOST SATISFACTIONS

Arthur Koestler's theory of bisociation appeared in an article by Tanneguy de Quénétain, "The Mechanics of Genius," which appeared in the January 1966 issue of *Realités* (p. 77). This magazine, renowned for its fine illustrations, is published in French and English editions. The English edition is cited here.

TACTIC FOUR: DEVELOP THE RESOURCES THAT COUNT

Money and Work

A great many old people do not realize that counseling help is readily available—whether counseling might involve coming to terms psychosocially with aging itself or specific financial planning. In a final section of this book (see the Appendix), I have listed several agencies to whom letters can be addressed for particular kinds of advice. I have also suggested literature that may be of assistance. Many colleges, businesses, and church groups now offer courses in retirement planning—often without charge.

Even those with very modest incomes would profit from a session with a good estate organizer or financial consultant long before retirement, but certainly it's better late than never. Reliable firms will not charge you for an initial visit, during which you can get some idea of what they can and cannot do for you. It's worth talking to several consultants before committing yourself to the guidance of any one person or firm. You may want to ask friends and professional acquaintances or your tax consultant what they do for assistance.

Physical and Mental Health

I am not sure I have emphasized enough how powerfully physical health is influenced by mental health. The older men and women who feel physically well are those who do not surrender to problems and who exert all possible effort to improve conditions, rather than wallow in the conviction that things will get worse. They are more inclined to be able to distinguish the onset of real illnesses that warrant medical attention from simple indulgence in self-pity or fatigue. They remain more active. They are inclined to eat well, exercise regularly, and sleep well. Consequently, they in fact tend to stay healthy. When sick, they monitor their condition with discretion and are better able to make informed judgments about just how much medical intervention is appropriate.

Many men and women over sixty seem to have lost contact with their bodies and would profit from a sober resolve to become more active and to feel the sense of aliveness that comes with making the most of one's body and one's mind. Books providing advice on age-appropriate exercises and activities are available in most bookstores and libraries. Before you begin any exercise program, however, be sure to consult your physician.

Some of the data on psychomotor performance contained in this chapter comes from *The Handbook of the Psychology of Aging* (James E. Birren and K. Warner Schaie. New York: Van Nostrand Reinhold, 1977).

According to the 1978 *Developments in Aging* report of the U.S. Senate, car ownership by the old is considerably below that of the young. A 1974 survey cited in this report shows that 62 per cent of older households owned at least one car, compared with 86 per cent in young (under-sixty-five) households. The difference, though, may be more a matter of income than of age, health, or choice; income level and car ownership are related at all age levels. In other words, the impoverished old often cannot afford to own automobiles (U.S. Senate, Special Committee on Aging, *Developments in Aging: 1978*, 96th Cong., 1st session, Rept. 96–55).

For detailed information on driving skills of old people see "Older Drivers' Record Good: They Face Fewer Road Hazards, Safety Council Reports" in the May 1969 issue of *Aging* (U.S. Department of Health, Education, and Welfare, Administration on Aging, p. 11).

Love and Sexuality

Kinsey's *Sexual Behavior in the Human Male* appeared a little over thirty years ago (A.C. Kinsey, W.B. Pomeroy, and C.E. Martin. Philadelphia: W.B. Saunders, 1948). Five years later his U.S.-based research report was extended to women subjects with the publication of *Sexual Behavior in the Human Female* (A.C. Kinsey, W.B. Pomeroy, C.E. Martin, and P.H. Gebhard. Philadelphia: W.B. Saunders, 1953).

For a review of current American sexual behavior and attitudes toward sex, see *Human Sexuality* (James L. McGary. 2nd Brief Edition; New York: D. Van Nostrand Co., 1979).

Human Sexual Response by William H. Masters and Virginia E. Johnson (Boston: Little, Brown, 1966) presented the first clinical analysis of the psychosexual responses of American men and women, documenting in detail their progression through four phases of the human sexual-response cycle.

A word of caution. After the publication in 1970 of Masters and Johnson's *Human Sexual Inadequacy* (Boston: Little, Brown)—a complex, highly detailed book—clinics specializing in sex therapy sprang up around the country. Clinics continue to grow in number: some are highly professional and are staffed by qualified therapists; many are not. Most are costly. In an effort to protect the public, The American Association of Sex Educators, Counselors, and Therapists enlisted a group of the nation's most respected and qualified professionals to establish guidelines for training and certification. That organization, AASECT, is the best-known (though unofficial) agency for certification of sex counselors and therapists. Men and women who would like the names of qualified persons to help them with sex-related counseling or who want to check the reliability of professionals in any part of the United States, should write to: AASECT, 5010 Wisconsin Avenue, N.W., Suite 304, Washington, D.C. 20016.

By far the most pertinent and sensitive discussion of the sexual needs of the elderly and how they can be met is contained in the sensitive and thorough *Love and Sex After Sixty: A Guide for Men and Women in Their Later Years* (Robert N. Butler and Myrna I. Lewis. New York: Harper & Row, 1977). An inexpensive book, it provides a fine guide for men and women in their later years and includes an excellent "Where To Go For Help" section.

The inward retreat that characterizes the psychosocial adjustment of some old persons who find themselves progressively divorced from human communication is something that Bernice Neugarten has called "the quality of interiority," an apt and rather poignant designation (in *Personality in Middle and Late Life*, in collaboration with Howard Berkowitz. New York: Atherton Press, 1964, p. 194).

TACTIC FIVE: DEVELOP THE ALLIANCES THAT COUNT

A Mate

In 1975 average life expectancy at birth was 68.7 years for men but almost eight years longer, or 76.5, for women. On the average, at age sixty-five men live 13.7 more years; women, 18 years. As a result of factors that are still largely unexplained, most older people are women. Specifically, between ages sixty-five and seventy-four there are 130 women per 100 men; after seventy-four, there are 176. Among the eighty-five-and-over, there are 217 women for every 100 men. (U.S. Senate, Special Committee on Aging, *Developments in Aging: 1977*, 95th Cong., 2d session, Rept. 95–771.)

The 1977 Senate report also points out that most older men are married (77 per cent), but most older women are widows (52 per cent). Of the seventy-five-plus women, almost 70 per cent are widows. Married men of sixty-five and over reflect the long-standing cultural consensus that women should be younger than their husbands: about 40 per cent of all surviving males over sixty-five have wives under sixty-five. First-marriage rates for older men are 7 times those for older women; for remarriages, 8.6 times.

The twenty-five-year increase in life expectancy since the beginning of this century has resulted from the eradication of diseases that earlier killed infants and children; it is much less a product of improvements in the chronic conditions and diseases that occur in upper-age groups.

Many more people now live to be sixty-five, but once at that age they live little longer (4.1 years) than did their ancestors. If cardiovascular disorders were reduced or brought under greater medical control, life expectancy in later years would be extended even more.

Projection of the numbers and proportion of old people shows continuing increases to the year 2000 and then very rapid growth from 2000 to 2025 as the postwar baby boom population becomes the aged population. Then there should be a sharp decline as the current low birthrates are reflected in the population pyramid.

Curiously, the traditionally rising proportion of women over men is predicted to be reversed in the years 2000 to 2025. Also, between now and 2000 the oldest (post-seventy-five) part of the population will grow most rapidly until, between 2000 and 2025, the current pattern is resumed with most (62.2 per cent) of the aged population under seventy-five and more than a third under seventy. To put all this in some perspective, it may be helpful to remember that when we discuss the elderly of 2025 we are discussing today's high school seniors!

Children and Grandchildren

Scotland, the Netherlands, Norway, Romania, Czechoslovakia, the USSR, and Japan generally have outstripped the United States in

219

the development of programs that help the old to help themselves and avoid dependency on children or institutional life. These countries are much more concerned with educating *all* adult men and women in the *prevention* of age-related problems through the training of geriatric specialists who are committed to helping patients take care of themselves. A strong effort is made to provide networks of assistance in times of crisis, in such forms as short-term domestic or nursing help, instruction *in the home* on the preparation of nutritious meals, and temporary hospitalization when necessary, with assistance in making a rapid return to home or apartment. Within our country comparable programs have been legislated, but they have been undermined by our failure to regard the old as a valid part of our communities.

Brothers and Sisters

A household survey cited in the 1978 Senate report showed that 13 in 100 persons aged sixty-five-plus had moved from one residence to another in the previous three years. In a pattern that has remained consistent for a long time, the majority of moves are close to previous homes, rarely beyond the county line, and in only 2.3 per cent of the cases, across the state line—and then to a very few states, principally Florida, Arizona, and Nevada.

Groups

At the end of this book is a list of some organizations for the aged (see the Appendix). Most are concerned with consciousness raising and effecting much-needed social changes. Many are excellent resource centers providing information and guidance of many kinds.

III A REVISED GAME PLAN: CREATING NEW GUIDELINES

Susan W. Byrne's account of life in a California adult-living community (Arden) appears in *Anthropologists in Cities* (Boston: Little, Brown, 1976).

Urgunge Onon's book, *My Childhood in Mongolia*, is one of a series on childhood (New York: Oxford University Press, 1972).

For a discussion of socioeconomic factors in aging, see Irving Rosow's *Social Integration of the Aged* (New York: Free Press, 1967).

George M. Foster has written extensively of Mexico and of the village of Tzintzuntzan. Observations on aging were a part of

Tzintzuntzan: Mexican Peasants in a Changing World (Boston: Little, Brown, 1967).

For an analysis of interpretations of late life in various societies around the world see the chapter, "Bioethics: Birth, Old Age, and Death" in *Medical Anthropology* (George M. Foster and Barbara Gallatin Anderson. New York: John Wiley & Sons, 1978).

The quotation by Margaret Mead is from "A Conversation with Margaret Mead and T. George Harris on the Anthropological Age," which appeared in the July 1970 issue of *Psychology Today* (p. 61). In the July 26, 1977 issue of *Family Circle* magazine, Grace Hechinger reports an absorbing interview with Margaret Mead on the occasion of her seventy-fifth birthday ("Growing Old in America," pp. 27–32). Margaret Mead took the opportunity to comment on the negative consequences of fear of aging and fear of the aged in the United States today; she also reminisces charmingly about her own grandmother.

According to the 1978 Senate report, voter participation falls off sharply after age seventy-five, which somewhat skews performance statistics for the group as a whole. In the 1976 election of President Jimmy Carter, older people made up 15 per cent of the voting age population. Approximately 62 per cent of the post-sixty-five population voted, a lower proportion than the thirty-five-to-sixty-four group, but higher than the under-thirty-five group. Women outnumbered men voters, but a greater *proportion* of older men than older women voted.

Appendix

GENERAL DISCUSSIONS OF AGING

Butler, Robert N. *Why Survive? Being Old in America.* New York: Harper & Row, 1975.
A book extraordinary enough to have won the 1976 Pulitzer Prize for nonfiction. The way life is and the way it can be for the aged. Written by a psychiatrist who is perhaps America's best authority on aging.

Comfort, Alex. *A Good Age.* New York: Simon & Schuster: 1978.
Designed to take the fear out of aging and to divest it of its many myths. You'll feel better for having read it.

Gross, Ronald; Gross, Beatrice; and Seidman, Sylvia. *The New Old: Struggling for Decent Aging.* Garden City, N.Y.: Doubleday, 1978.
A provocative anthology of writings by Margaret Mead, Maggie Kuhn (Gray Panthers), Robert Butler, Alex Comfort, Juanita Kreps, and others. Includes a fine section on books, organizations, and services that provide resources and help for the elderly.

Hendricks, John, and Hendricks, C. Davis. *Aging in Mass Society: Myths and Realities.* Englewood Cliffs, N.J.: Winthrop Publishers, Inc., 1977.
Myths and realities of aging: psychological processes, health, work and retirement, family life, politics, minority status.

Heavy-going, but informative. Deals almost exclusively with the U.S.

U.S., Congress, Senate, Special Committee on Aging. *Developments in Aging* (Parts 1 and 2).
Published annually. Part 1 is probably the most useful; Part 2 is a collection of appendixes to Part 1. Both have comprehensive tables of contents. Available through your library or the U.S. Government Printing Office, Washington, D.C. Price varies annually.

AGING IN OTHER CULTURES

The selections marked with asterisks are as easy to read as they are informative; the others are more academic in their approach.

* Benet, Sula. *Abkhasians: The Long-Living People of the Caucasus.* New York: Holt, Rinehart and Winston, 1974.

* Coles, Robert. *The Old Ones of New Mexico.* Garden City, N.Y.: Doubleday, 1975.

Cowgill, Donald O., ed. *Aging and Modernization.* New York: Appleton-Century-Crofts, 1972.
Articles by sociologists and anthropologists on aging in Ethiopia, Africa, Samoa, Thailand, Mexico, Ireland, Austria, Israel, and Norway, as well as the United States.

* Kramer, Sydelle, and Masur, Jenny. *Jewish Grandmothers.* Boston: Beacon Press, 1976.

* Leaf, Alexander, and Launois, John. *Youth in Old Age.* New York: McGraw-Hill, 1975.
The impact of this book lies in its rich supply of photographs of old people in remote regions of the world. These are linked to an analysis of the factors that contribute to long, healthy, active, and productive lives.

* Matthiasson, Carolyn J., ed. *Many Sisters: Women in Cross-Cultural Perspective.* New York: Free Press, 1974.
Not limited to aging, but relevant. How it feels to live as a woman in Peru, Egypt, France, Guatemala, India, Nigeria, China, and other countries. Photographs.

Ross, Jennie-Keith. *Old Peoples, New Lives: Community Creation in a Retirement Residence.* Chicago: University of Chicago Press, 1977.
Life in a French retirement residence.

Shanas, Ethel, and Streib, Gordon. *Old People in Three Industrial Societies.* New York: Atherton Press, 1968.
Aging in Britain, Denmark, and the United States.

Smith, Robert J. "Cultural Differences in the Life Cycle and the Concept of Time." In *Aging and Leisure,* edited by Robert W. Kleemeier. New York: Oxford University Press, 1961.
Fascinating accounts of aging in the Andes, among Eskimo, Japanese, Burmans, and in Indian society.

ADVICE: GENERAL AND SPECIFIC

Butler, Robert N., and Lewis, Myrna I. *Love and Sex After Sixty.* New York: Harper & Row, 1977.
A definitive, explicit, caring guide for men and women in their later years. Both a text on late-life sex and a gentle how-to book. Everything you ever wanted to know about sex after sixty but were afraid to ask. Inexpensive and well-written.

Fraser, Virginia, and Thornton, Susan M. *The New Elders: Innovative Programs by, for, and about the Elderly.* Denver: Loretto Heights College, 1977.
Information about fifty programs available to the aged in the U.S. today. Will give you a feel for the quality and direction of current activities.

Hunter, Woodrow W. *Preparation for Retirement.* 3rd ed. Institute of Gerontology, University of Michigan. Detroit: Wayne State University Press, 1976.
Considers problems of postemployment years.

Romney, Leonard S., and Hoffman, Lee A., Jr. *Advocacy Handbook for Senior Citizens.* Albany, N.Y.: State University of New York Press, 1976.
The message here is: senior citizens, your future is in your hands, and this is the guidebook to action. A clear account of the rights of the elderly and how to make the most of them.

Stonecypher, D.D., Jr. *Getting Older and Staying Young.* New York: W.W. Norton, 1974.
A doctor's prescription for continuing vitality in later life.

The following are some of the major organizations with nationwide membership and periodicals designed to keep the old abreast of age-oriented legislation, programs, conferences, special opportunities, news, and other information.

American Association of Retired Persons
1909 K Street, N.W.
Washington, D.C. 20049

> Works closely with the National Retired Teachers Association to improve the quality of life for old people.

Gray Panthers
3700 Chestnut Street
Philadelphia, Pennsylvania 19104

> Reform-oriented activists, striving to end age discrimination and improve the quality of life for the old. The vitality of the organization has promoted the rapid growth of fifty-eight local chapters.

National Council of Senior Citizens
1511 K Street, N.W.
Washington, D.C. 20005

> Affiliates over 3,500 senior citizen clubs. Advises Congress on problems facing the elderly and recommends approaches to their resolution. A good resource for answers to age-related questions on local, state, or national level.

National Council on the Aging
1828 L Street, N.W.
Washington, D.C. 20036

> Works principally as as a resource center for professionals and in the development of programs that meet the changing needs of the elderly. Concerned in part with the reeducation of the general public to a more supportive view of the aged population.

Administration on Aging
Office of Human Development
U.S. Department of Health, Education, and Welfare
330 Independence Avenue, S.W.
Washington, D.C. 20201

> Headed by Dr. Robert N. Butler and charged with administration of the Older Americans Act. Enormously important on an advo-

cacy level in many facets of federal planning, particularly in interdepartmental coordination. May provide the stature and influence necessary to exert sweeping changes in the condition of the old.

Write any and all of the above for assistance on specific questions. If they cannot provide the answer, they will guide you in finding it. Most have modest membership fees. All have periodicals.

Information and assistance within your state:

Over 500 area agencies and 800 nutrition-project agencies have been established by the Administration on Aging. This network, which now reaches eight out of ten persons over the age of sixty-five, was established by Congress in response to the Older Americans Act of 1973. The proliferation of services designed to meet priorities established by the various states represents one of the most significant advances in the field of aging in recent years. The address of your nearest commission or office or division on aging (the titles unfortunately are not uniform) concerned with services for the aged can be obtained by writing the Administration on Aging (address given above). In many states the address and phone number are listed in your local telephone directory along with other state agencies. Write or phone "The Director."

CASUAL READING

Where the aged are a part of fiction it is all too often as the equivalent of what Hollywood calls "character actors." They are the quaint or besotted sidekicks of heroes, avaricious financiers, meddling mothers-in-law, kindly old physicians or strict teachers, the heroine's foreign-born parents, child-frightening recluses, or endearingly grumpy grandparents. They are rarely the protagonists of stories and, more rarely still, individuals whose life styles we envy. Two delightful exceptions in recent fiction are Dorothy Gilman's Mrs. Pollifax (perhaps too intrepid) and Agatha Christie's Miss Marple. Adventure and romance periodically enliven Mrs. Pollifax's seemingly prosaic existence, and both ladies have proved the intellectual match of many a villain and are stalwart enough for some demanding skirmishes. Hemingway created some powerful old men, but as characters they seem to incorporate more of the frustrations than challenges of old age, reflecting perhaps Hemingway's own terror of aging. Nevertheless, his *The Old Man and The Sea* makes memorable reading, as does James Hilton's *Goodbye, Mr. Chips*.

One of the best nonscholarly, nonfiction treatments of old people in recent years is Sharon B. Curtin's *Nobody Ever Died of Old Age,* a collection of vignettes "in praise of old people . . . in outrage at their loneliness . . ." (Boston: Little, Brown, 1973).

Index

233

237

238